a small ray of light

a small ray of light

John Egbert Turner

Copyright © 1977   John E. Turner
ISBN 0-919654-97-5

> Cataloging in Publication Data
>
> Turner, John Egbert.
>   A small ray of light
>
> ISBN 0-919654-97-5
>
>   1. Philosophical anthropology.
>   2. Life on other planets. I. Title.
> BD450.T87   128   C77-002104-2

All rights reserved. No part of this publication may be reproduced, stored in a retrieval system or transmitted, in any form or by any means, electronic, mechanical, photocopying, recording or otherwise, without the prior written permission of Hancock House Publishers.

PRINTED IN CANADA

Published by:

Hancock House Publishers Ltd.
3215 Island View Road
SAANICHTON, B.C. V0S 1M0

Hancock House Publishers Inc.
12008 1st Avenue South
SEATTLE, WA. 98168

CONTENTS

1. A Few Introductory Remarks .. 9
2. The Possibility of Complete Mind Reading 16
3. Human Intelligence and Morality 23
4. Intelligent Life Elsewhere in the Universe 41
5. What We Can Expect of the Future..................... 61
6. Some Thoughts on Religion... 86
7. What We Can do Now 101

Preface

My purpose in writing this little book is to make an attempt at showing that the time has come for a beginning to be made in the abandonment of all religious beliefs and their replacement by conclusions based on intelligence, reason and logic. I try to explain how the latter, while not requiring anything to be accepted on nothing more than mere faith, can, and I am convinced, will supply us with everything promised by religion.

This dissertation could, I suppose be characterized by the proverb, "Fools rush in where angels fear to tread." I consider myself to be a man whose education has been minimal: but I maintain that this very lack of education is, in some ways an advantage in this particular case. Every small plateau attained in our slow and tedious upward climb toward a better society will, as has been the case in the past, be achieved by those most learned and skilled in each particular field; and I acknowledge that each individual involved in such advances is much more important to the human race than I. My contention is that one so deeply occupied in any of the numerous fields, the immediate difficulties loom so tremendously large as to preclude any reasonable possibility of assessing far distant goals, and the methods by which they may eventually be reached.

I first became interested in the likelihood of intelligent life at other places in the universe some fifty years ago, and since that time I have been attracted and absorbed by anything related to the subject, also by anything at all related to the ultimate destiny of man, both individually and collectively. During this half century I have become increasingly fascinated by the possibilities inherent in the things which I have learned. I do not mean to imply that this has been a lifetime work; it has been however, an absorbing avocation.

More than thirty years ago I came to the reluctant decision that I should put my thoughts on paper, but this painful process was not actually started until some twenty years later. Had this been done by a writer of greater talent, the difficulties would probably have proven to be not excessive, but for one such as myself the task turned out to be nothing less than herculean.

The process of making notes and writing bits and pieces began in the year 1962 and was carried on sporadically since that time. Following my retirement in 1972 I have devoted much more time to it, especially during the last year. I have now finally brought the project to a conclusion. Whatever success I may have had in this endeavor I'll leave for others to judge.

Every thinking person will agree, I am sure, that the highest aspiration any of us can have is to leave this world, in some slight way, better than we found it because of our having lived here for a time. This little work I consider to be my chief effort in that direction. I only wish that it could have been more.

                        John Egbert Turner,
                        Vancouver, B.C.

1 A Few Introductory Remarks

Before getting the reader involved in my various discussions concerning the probable future of our race, there are a few points which I feel should be clarified in order to save him some possible confusion.

In attempting to assess our far distant possibilities I have assumed that our race is the first group of intelligent beings to have come into existence, or at least the only such group which has survived and is continuing to grow at the present time. However, let me hasten to add that in my opinion any such assumption is as preposterous as the view held in ancient times that our earth was the exact center of the entire universe.

My reason for temporarily taking this obviously false position is that I am attempting to determine the utmost advancements which might be made by a group such as ourselves provided that they had sufficient time, luck and initiative. To me it seems obvious that an enormous number—in all likelihood approaching an infinite number—of such intelligent groups have arisen during past eons, and that a large number of them have long since attained the absolute state of development and, as must necessarily follow, have since remained and will for all time continue in that happy position.

Obviously it would be much more difficult to assess the

possibility of any such ultra-super civilization without referring to our own race in its present state of early infancy. It seems to me that by far the best method of attempting to resolve this question is to look to ourselves and to determine what our future would be, supposing that we were the first group of intelligent beings to arise in the entire cosmos, and provided that we continue to progress in a manner somewhat as I outline in the following chapters.

Any or all of my theories and speculations may be greatly in error as of detail, but I am quite firmly convinced that many developments such as I envisage have taken place during the vast number of bygone ages. I do not see how it could have been otherwise. This being the case, our wanderings through space for hundreds of billions of years, upon which I speculate, would be unnecessary—at least finding our own way and constantly groping for new and essential knowledge would be unnecessary—as we would, long before that time, be given the needed help and guidance by those who had gone before. I have not the slightest doubt that events such as these have taken place a very great many times in the past with help given to groups similar to ourselves but in a much more advanced state of development.

This brings up the question concerning the position which we must achieve before any such help may be expected and as to when it may be forthcoming. I can only say that in my opinion we should not look for any such assistance until every last lowly member of our race has achieved the ethical standards of the greatest of all our saint-like persons, past or present.

It will be when we have become a race of human beings, rather than one of a slightly higher order of animals which we are at present. As to the time required for this advancement, my guess (and of course it is only a guess) is that it might be something in the order of one or two millenniums. We have a great distance to go.

During the last half of the 1970 s, reports of a rather fantastic nature have been made public concerning experiences of various persons during periods of a few minutes duration between their seeming death and their subsequent resuscitation. During this short time these people showed all of the normal indications of death, including complete cessation of respiration and heart action, and would have most certainly been declared irrevocable dead by the world's most eminent medical authorities up until only a few years ago. Following their revival and return to consciousness, these people—at least those about whom I have seen reports—relate somewhat similar experiences. First is a feeling of well-being; not only complete freedom from any pain, discomfort and anxiety which they may have had, but also a sense of great relief from the weight of life itself, together with a sensation of exhilaration to an extent previously quite unknown. Second is a realization of great light and a sureness that they have the ability to understand things which had been previously quite incomprehensible. I have not heard of any of them expanding on this point and explaining various mysteries following their return to consciousness, but possibly this could be expecting altogether too much and it is likely that they had only the sensation of understanding. On the other hand there is the possibility that during these brief periods they were on a mental plane so much higher than ours that, even supposing they retained this great understanding, we would be far short of the ability needed to grasp any such explanations: but it is most probable that any such capability of theirs would be lost upon their return. Third, and most important, is a feeling of reality. If all of these experiences were, as might be expected, nothing more than sensations of a dying mind, then reality would be about the last thing which I would expect. A more reasonable expectation would be the type of mental activity we have all encountered during periods of delirium which tend to accompany serious illnesses, or in ordinary hazy and only fractionally recalled dreams. The most common characteristic of such mental aberrations as these is fuzziness, certainly not reality.

My first inclination regarding these accounts of experiences under such unusual circumstances is to discard them outright as fiction (either intentional or otherwise) of a religious sentimentalist. This I have not done, and I am mentioning them here for two principle reasons. The first of these is that they do not in the least conform to the standards of such religious twaddle as we have all been exposed to on many occasions. Second, and more important is that at least two such accounts were given by individuals of the highest credibility. The first of these was the talented and eminently successful fiction writer, W. Somerset Maugham. The other was an even more illustrious man, Dr. Carl Gustav Jung who was, of course, one of those who laid the foundations for the practice of psychiatry. Both of these must be considered entirely reliable witnesses, and not in the least given to inventing sentimental rubbish. For this reason I must take seriously accounts of that nature, although I am not in any way taking it upon myself to pass judgment as to whether such experiences have any real significance.

It may be of some slight interest to know that the main body of this work was completed more than a year prior to the writing of these introductory remarks, and before any of these unusual accounts had come to my attention. A secondary reason for mentioning them is to point out that the following chapters outline a satisfactory—at least to me—explanation as to how these occurrences could be possible without the aid of anything of a supernatural or miraculous nature. A further reason, and one of lesser importance, has to do with an interesting point about which to speculate. There are some persons who accept the recounting of these experiences as proof positive that at least some members of our race are, at the very moment of death, taken into a life of a much higher order. I am not one of these. I do no more than admit the possibility. But let me presume for the moment that they are completely right in this assertion, and that following immediately the instant of death, some of us, or possibly most of us, or even all of us are transported into a new and better life. This knowledge would not be particularly surprising to me in view of the conclusions I have reached and which are mentioned later in this discourse. What I would find somewhat astounding is that this disclosure had been given to us at such an early stage of our development. I would have been disinclined to expect anything of this nature for at least another several centuries.

Taking into account all of the conclusions which I have felt compelled to accept during my many years of speculation on these subjects, I have to admit to the existence of a supreme power. I contend that this omnipotence (or close approximation thereof) is composed of an extremely large number—possibly something approaching an infinite number—of individuals who make up the total included in all of the civilizations which have reached the ultimate in development; and that all of these individuals work together in a state of harmony entirely beyond our comprehension. I take it as obvious that this supreme entity was not the creator of the universe, but rather the logical and inevitable outgrowth of its environment. As it is almost certain that the cosmos is infinite, it follows that this supreme power comes close to that state.

It will be noticed here, as in many other places in my discussions, I have tossed around the word "infinite" with some abandon, and as though I knew what it meant—which, of course, I do not. It would be quite easy to substitute another word such as "endless", "everlasting" or "unlimited", but to do so would merely be to exchange one mystery for another. To put the same thing another way could be to ask: What are the final limits of time and space? In this connection, whether time and space are, or are not the same thing in the final analysis, is immaterial.

Admission of the existence of a supreme entity brings up questions for which answers have been sought since the dawn of history. Such questions are as numerous and as varied in form as are the persons or groups eagerly seeking answers. But practically all of them seem to arise from one main focal point, and may be summed up in a general way somewhat as follows; assuming, as we must, that a continuous stream of new life is, and has been arising over an infinite period of time, then we must admit that all desirable life has long since been created and that we are now in a constant process of being recycled. Why is this being done? What useful purpose can be served by periodically subjecting every individual, each of whom is presumably a part of the supreme entity, to all the horrors of this life? There have been many attempts at answering this connundrum which have been posed in diverse manners. The only thing that can be said for these explanations is that they serve only to confuse an already hopelessly muddled issue. For instance, there is the case of the three-headed god. These heads represent the creator, the preserver and the destroyer. The explanation here is that this three-in-one god constantly creates and destroys for "sport". Any such philosphy must be rejected out of hand as being too preposterous to merit even the slightest consideration.

It is altogether likely that there are quite logical answers to all of these questions, but even supposing that they were supplied to us, we do not at present have anything approaching sufficient intellect to make possible any understanding of them. A similar situation could be that of a professor attempting to instruct his dog in higher mathematics. It is not unreasonable to suppose that we have about as far to go as has this professor's dog.

For us, in our present state of development, these and kindred matters must be regarded as being beyond our comprehension, and should be set aside for the present and for the foreseeable future. Until such time as our intellectual capacities have increased manyfold beyond their present state, I would most earnestly suggest that we confine our attention to matters about which we have at least a little understanding. We should make every effort to increase our knowledge and skills in the widest possible range of fields to the fullest possible extent. At the same time, and of much more importance, is the need to raise our ethical standards to a position where we might be considered a truly civilized society and one which might be deemed worthy of outside assistance from distant life far superior to ourselves. When that time arrives such help will be forthcoming.

2 The Possibility of Complete Mind Reading

Sometime during the 1950s I read an article concerning the possibility of the existence of intelligent life elsewhere than on this little planet of ours. The only thing about this item which I retained was a rather sarcastic observation that a few rather dull individuals seemed to hold the opinion that these super-creatures possess powers of an awesome nature. Some of those holding this view, the writer observed, went to the length of making the outlandish suggestion that these beings, aided by apparatus of intricacy beyond our wildest imagination, might have the ability while hovering near our earth to read the innermost minds of each of us.

At the moment I do not concern myself with the existence or non-existence of such beings. As a matter of fact I cannot see any solid reason for doubting their existence. But my concern now is with the speculation about looking into minds.

As a comparison to the above indirect quotation, a well considered statement, culminating from much serious thought on the matter, might well have been made some three or four centuries ago by a leading scientist of that time, as follows: "There has recently been some talk among the addle-brained and unknowing elements of our society concerning the possibility at some time in the remote future, of human transportation by means of some sort of mechanical contrivance. Some of the more completely irresponsible of these visionaries make so bold as to go to the utterly absurd lengths of predicting that man may, in some future century, find means of propelling himself at the ungodly rate of sixty miles per hour. Those of us of a more sober and serious turn of mind have little time and less sympathy for such impossible fantasies, and are not inclined to take seriously such idiotic pipe dreams."

My purpose in making this comparison is simply to stress the fact that man has always tended to underestimate his own abilities. I do not mean to imply any underestimation of his present abilities, but only those of the more or less distant future. This is important to me for the reason that the purpose of this discourse is to attempt an evaluation of the ultimate ability of mankind and to chart some kind of rough course which may eventually be of some slight help in guiding the human race toward a higher level of attainment; and also in using whatever little influence I may have in an effort toward steering present thought into that direction.

Of prime importance in this matter is the question of whether it will become possible at some extremely distant time, to look into and to completely record the human mind. When we consider a task of this magnitude we must think in terms of the potentialities of a civilization which has attained its ultimate development. I quite realize the utter impossibility of any such accomplishment within the reasonably foreseeable future.

Here I am reminded of a conversation in which I took part when I was twelve years old. This conversation was of what I suppose could be called a trivial nature but for some reason it has remained in my memory. This occurred at a time when I was visiting at the home of an elderly lady who was some kind of a relation. Somehow a reference was made to the old saw, "Time and tide wait for no man." I mentioned that I could understand the impossibility of man ever controlling time, but that I could not quite put tide into the same category as it seemed to me that it might indeed prove to be controllable by man at some distant time. This brought forth the question from this sweet old lady, "Could you do it?" I had to admit that I could not. With a tolerant smile she muttered some sort of monosyllable which seemed to indicate that she was completely satisfied at having very gently put me in my place and had routed me in the debate. I did not pursue the matter, but I thought that her reasoning was, to say the least, faulty. That is, if a boy of twelve is unable to accomplish some particular task, then it must remain forever impossible. I might have pointed out that I was also quite incapable of pulling a freight train over the mountains from Calgary to Vancouver, and yet that very thing was being done several times every day.

When I consider the recording of a human mind I am thinking, as mentioned above, of a time when the human race has advanced to a point where it is close to the ultimate in intelligence and ability, or when we have advanced down that road to a point where we are worthy enough and have sufficient capabilities of receiving help from another source. If left to our own resources—which I consider highly unlikely—I would envisage this time as being probably some hundreds of millenniums in the future. When we consider the attainments of certain abilities at that time we must think, not in terms of what is known now, but in terms of what is physically possible. When looked at in this way, it would seem that there are very few things which we must consider to be forever beyond our capabilities. During my considerations as to the possibility of completely recording human minds, had I been able to find some solid reason that this must be forever outside of our power, then there would have been no point in my continuing with this work. I propose, at this time to follow my line of reasoning which has led me to the conclusion that such recording must eventually be entirely possible.

Having in this way somewhat outlined my perspective, let me return to my deliberations of mind reading. At first glance most of us are inclined to regard mind reading as a sort of pseudo-science; something from the realm of fairy tales, having no place in actual human experience, past, present or future. In actual fact it is nothing of the sort. Each of us does it to some extent every day—excepting those days when we are isolated from others of our kind.

If I look at another person even casually, I am able to discern certain obvious things about his present state of mind. For instance, whether or not he is angry, fearful, jealous, elated, or bored. This much may be determined at a glance by almost any person with a modicum of intelligence and perception. A longer and more careful look will reveal correspondingly more depending on the skill and knowledge of the viewer. It might be observed whether he is languid, placid and stolid or extremely alert, or inclined toward nervous tension; whether he is given to self-indulgence or to rigid self-discipline. These and many other indications of his mental condition and background may be apparent. Such things are not usually thought of as mind reading, but that is exactly what they are—mind reading of a very low order of course, but mind reading nevertheless.

At this point two questions arise: what are the ultimate limits of mind reading, and what limits are imposed by distance? Although I feel that the question of distance will eventually prove to be of no great importance, still, it may be worth a brief examination. Just what difficulties are placed in the way of such crude and elementary powers as I possess, by the subject being removed from me by one hundred feet, by several hundreds of miles, or by hundreds of thousands of miles? On first thought it might be supposed that as soon as he is separated from me by as much as one hundred feet, then my ability to determine anything at all about his mental state is entirely lost. But suppose that I have a good pair of binoculars: with their help he again becomes as visible to me as when he was no further away than three of four feet. My mind reading ability has been fully restored. It is clear then that the question of distance resolves itself into one of visibility, and if sufficient visibility is established then distance makes no difference whatever. Obviously then, any space men hovering a few hundred miles, or for that matter many thousands of miles outside of our atmosphere would not be hampered in their efforts to look into our minds by the mere fact that they are some distance away. What we are concerned with is the limiting factor of power and clarity of telescopes. Are there actually any ultimate limiting problems?

We are disposed to think of the maximum in telescopes as the two-hundred-inch model now in use on top of Mount Palomar in California. A century or two ago a six-inch model may well have been regarded in the same light. These two are quite similar in every respect with the exception of size. Up to the present time very little basic change has been made, and it may be true that no fundamentally new approach to this science is technically possible yet. But surely this is not true for all time. It is quite inconceivable that this science has already reached its final attainment at this very early date in the history of science. It would seem apparent that this, in common with so many other human skills, is still in its earliest infancy.

I am inclined to visualize the ultimate in telescopes as a device located well out beyond the earth's atmosphere and spanning an enormous area. It would ignore light coming from our sun or any other source where there was at the time no interest, but would pick up all light required of it, including the rays of smallest magnitude as well as those which have been travelling through empty space for billions of years. Also included would be all radiated energy from the source under study whether or not it fell within the narrow spectrum of visible radiation. Each of the smallest units of this radiated energy would be recorded individually and fed into some sort of a sorting and categorizing device which would assemble them in useful form. The difficulties in the way of this development are, at the present time, quite insurmountable, but in years to come I am convinced they will become increasingly less so.

I now propose to examine the more intriguing and more important question, namely: What, if any, are the ultimate limitations of looking into a human mind by any means whatever, including radiation—light or otherwise, and reflected or otherwise—and by any other means about which present knowledge is limited or non-existent.

As I have pointed out, and is indeed self-evident, when one such as myself, of no more than average intelligence and with no particular skill in such matters, looks at another person, then some information is gained regarding the other person's mental make-up. The amount of this fragmentary information is, of course very small and is subject to error, but still it adds up to at least a little knowledge. Let us suppose now that my skill in this matter were to be increased. This could, no doubt be done by study, by getting instructions from those better versed in the matter and by diligent and constant practice. The increase in my skill could be limited by only two things; the extent of my native intelligence, and the time factor, i.e.; the loss of my mental facilities through illness, senility or death. But for as long as my skill actually does continue to increase then surely the results must continue to increase in some sort of ratio thereto. During my short lifetime it is possible for me to increase my skill in this art by only an insignificant degree.

There are prospects amounting to virtual certainty that both limitations will eventually be removed. Provided that mankind overcomes its present asinine inclination toward self-destruction, and that its present rate of progress in less insane directions is maintained, then it is almost certain that during the coming centuries human intelligence and the human life span will be increased to a point where they will begin to approach the infinite. With the removal of these restrictions, infinite intelligence and skill can be brought to bear on this important problem by the human race. When infinite skill is brought to bear on a finite problem—one not physically impossible of solution—then the result must eventually be a completely resolved problem.

Before leaving this subject I would like to mention another possible means of getting information concerning the human brain. The method which suggests itself is that of sending agents into the brain in question. It may not be impossible for these to be living intelligent beings, but scaled down temporarily to extremely small proportions for this particular job; but this need not necessarily be the case, as they could be entirely inanimate objects. A similarity to a present practice could be that of putting a very small—by our standards—television camera into some place where visibility is not feasible by any other means, such as the bottom of an oil well, in order to gain information not available in other ways. I would think that it is quite conceivable that some such method as this could yield information complementing that which is obtained by other methods, or perhaps even supplanting it. It is not beyond imagination that some process of this sort is going on within the head of each of us continuously, and about which we are, obviously, quite unaware. It may well be that as I sit here writing these words there are numerous agents of this kind busily at work inside my head.

To get back to the suggestion of a group of beings superior to ourselves having the ability to look into our innermost minds, I cannot see that they should have any particular difficulty in doing this if such should be their desire. I do not mean to imply that any intelligent life necessarily has this ability merely because it is able to accomplish interstellar travel. It is entirely possible that this type of travelling might be done by a race which, although a great deal more accomplished than we are at the present time, is still far from having reached its ultimate goals. When I suggest the possibility of some race from a distance far beyond our little solar system being able to analyze us thoroughly and completely at this moment, I am assuming that they have developed to a degree where they have reached their final goals.

3 Human Intelligence

During the last thirty or so years a great many statements have been made and opinions advanced concerning the likelihood of an invasion and conquest of this world by some sort of super-creatures from some place beyond the confines of this planet. These opinions seem to have been issued with the fond hope, and indeed the expectation that they would be regarded as profound and well reasoned results of long and careful study of the matter. I am sure that I have neither read nor heard all of them by any means, but those which have come to my attention I am inclined to regard as silly and fallacious. Most of the proponents of these opinions seem to take it for granted that these beings would have all of our vices and none of our virtues. Their main concern appears to be: "How can we best defend ourselves against these vile monsters?" One writer made the suggestion that should we be foolish enough to allow ourselves to fall into their power, we could expect that in all probability we would be used for the same purpose as that for which we use our cattle. At that, it seems to me, we would have small grounds for complaint of unjust treatment.

Those making statements of this kind seem to base their conclusions on whatever knowledge they may have of human conquerors since the dawn of history. They probably have in mind such as the early Norsement, Attila the Hun, Genghis

Khan, Napoleon and Hitler. Judged superficially, the centuries would seem to have brought very little improvement.

One writer went to a different kind of extreme. He credited these invaders with good intentions but with utterly incredible gullibility and stupidity. These implications were made in a radio play broadcast by the C.B.C., sometime during the early 1950s. The title of this play, if I recall it correctly was, *The Day of the Flying Saucer.* As I remember it, the plot went something like this:

A huge object of strange appearance, completely unlike anything ever seen before by human eyes, appeared in the sky over Lake Ontario. It settled down to hover a few hundred feet above the water at a point a few miles offshore from Toronto. Great consternation resulted among the local inhabitants, and within a few hours became national in scope. No governmental official at any level had the slightest clue as to the manner in which a situation of this type should be handled. It was obviously going to take considerable time before a decision could be reached as to just what, if any, action should be taken. As things transpired this delay turned out to be disasterous.

While there was no immediate decision forthcoming from a high level, a plan for fast action was put into effect at a very low level without any delay whatever. It consisted of a lone junior member of the R.C.A.F. jumping into his plane, and, presumably, without the knowledge of his superiors, and in the best Saint George tradition, went forth to do battle with the "enemy".

This act of heroism was plainly against what in all common sense should have been overwhelming odds. Common sense however, would appear to have no place in this great piece of fiction.

The occupants of the "Flying Saucer" were evidently quite unprepared for even the puniest attack; and their spaceship turned out to be as fragile, awkward and vulnerable as if it had been a hydrogen-filled dirigible of 1919 vintage. After a few quick passes by our hero with machine guns blazing, it was all over and the spaceship fell to the water in flames and sank with all hands into the presumably unfathomable depths of Lake Ontario. This development was to the great dismay of all right thinking persons including the author of this silly tale. The implied message seemed to be: "What a hell of a way to treat friendly callers!!"

The above account puts these spacemen into about the same category as a small group of singularly stupid Canadian missionaries who, some years ago decided to bring the benefits of Christianity to a tribe of natives somewhere on the upper reaches of the Amazon River. This tribe was, and still is, as far as I know, noted for its brutal viciousness, its savagery and its treachery. These were the citizens of a village which our little band of over zealous and not-too-bright missionaries decided to penetrate. They proceeded upon this venture with outstretched hands of friendship after having persuaded each other that if they approached these natives peacefully, without anything which could be mistaken for an offensive weapon, and armed only with gifts, good intentions and prayers, they would be received with kindness and gracious hospitality. The upshot of the affair was that about half of their number, upon walking into the village were forthwith entrapped and butchered, The surviving members beat a hasty retreat, and have since confined their soul-saving ardor to other parts of the world where the population is somewhat less inclined to unfriendliness. I cannot take it to be anything less than an absolute certainty that any possible space visitors to this world would know exactly what kind of a reception to expect, and that any attack which we could mount against them, either individually or collectively, would be notably unsuccessful. Stupidity is one quality which will not, we may be quite sure, apply to them. It must be self-evident that any living beings who arrive here from interstellar space must, by the very fact that they have successfully made such a journey, be of an extremely high order of intelligence, at least when judged by our criteria.

While it may be a fairly simple matter to establish the level of intelligence of such visitors, what is not so easily prophesied is their probably standard of ethics. Most of the expressed opinions appear to have been based on the assumption, without any stated reason, that they would be about equal to those of Genghis Khan or Hitler. I have always felt, rather instinctively, that these views are entirely in error and are arrived at partly from a too casual examination of historical events, or—and much more importantly—by looking at history from a distorted viewpoint. We have, of course, no evidence upon which to form a judgment, except that which we can gather from our own past. Nevertheless, before proceeding to see what can be learned from that source, I would like to say that had it been necessary for me to form a conclusion from within a complete vacuum, it would be that, by and large, high intelligence and high ethical standards must inevitably go together.

This brings me to the matter which I set out to explore: the relationship between the improvement in human intelligence and the improvement in human ethical standards during recorded history. No possible doubt can be entertained as to the growth of our knowledge and intelligence throughout the centuries since they both started from zero several millions of years ago. As far as knowledge itself is concerned, its advancement during recorded history, say the last four thousand years, has been the more notable of the two. The statement has been made—and not, to my knowledge at least, seriously disputed—that in the field of science generally more progress was made during the first half of this century than in all previous history. I have not heard of this matter being discussed since the statement which I refer to was made shortly after the middle of the century, but it would seem safe to assume that there has been no slackening in this rate of progress during the 24 years up to the present.

Human intelligence cannot be referred to in exactly the same way, although I do not see how its advancement, past and present, can be doubted. In any case I do not propose to debate the point. My whole purpose is to make the best prediction of which I am capable, concerning the ultimate destiny of the entire race, either with or without—but almost certainly with—assistance from other intelligent life. In this connection I am inclined to take for granted the progress of our intelligence and knowledge. However, the question of advancement of our ethics is another matter and is indeed all important.

I am definitely of the opinion, as I will try to show, that our morality has advanced during recorded history, and that it is at present advancing, and will continue to advance, subject to occasional backsliding. I hold the opinion also, as would seem to be an obvious conclusion, that a high level of moral and ethical standards is bound to be present with intelligent life anywhere.

Incalculable suffering, misery, bloodshed and havoc were recently inflicted upon the human race by the infamous Hitler. In the minds of a great many notable people whose opinions have been given publicity, the events chargeable to his evil genius loom large enough to make any suggestion of improvement in ethics since our earliest history appear completely ridiculous. These opinions have my complete understanding and sympathy; but at the same time, and with all due deference to the honest convictions of these people, I believe that they are mistaken. In my judgment, they are led into the obvious error by a false perspective from which they are comparing near events to distant events.

A fairly complete and accurate description of Hitler could be made with equal conviction and truthfulness about hundreds of previous characters. Hitler outdid all of his predecessors in infamy only in the magnitude of his crimes and in the sheer numbers of lives lost due to his degraded activities. A few minutes reflection should convince any reasonable person that the manner in which he excelled was not in any way due to a higher moral standard on the part of his nefarious forerunners, but merely to greater opportunities accounted for entirely by advancement in science, and in its application to warfare and other evil deeds. In exactly the same way a present-day Hitler probably could and most surely would, a mere thirty years later, wipe humanity entirely from the face of the earth without the slighest compunction, when his defeat became imminent. In all periods of history there have been, just as in all probability there will continue to be for a considerable time in the future, those who are more than eager to gain some slight advantage for themselves at the cost of a terrible amount of human suffering. This is a fact of life to which we must reconcile ourselves for more than a few generations to come. It is the responsibility of the rest of us to see that these vile geniuses do not gain control.

In assessing any possible gain in our ethical standards over the centuries, it is only natural that we should compare Hitler—and all the little Hitlers and would-be Hitlers—with their predecessors as far back as our records go. I am quite sure that this comparison does not supply us with the most reliable answers; nevertheless, I feel that if we are absolutely objective about it, this madman would show up to a slight advantage. There is no doubt that he made every attempt to exterminate whole races of people, and even enjoyed doing so. In his evil mind, he deemed it to be nothing less than his sacred duty, and something which would eventually work toward the betterment of humanity, in exactly the same manner in which a farmer might regard the extermination of pests. As is to be expected in one of his kind, there is no doubt that he derived sadistic pleasure in torturing these unfortunate people, as he most certainly did in torturing those who he believed to be traitors to his cause, or those who were stubborn obstacles to his ambitions, the fulfilment of which would, in his insane way of thinking, justify any means whatever. Some ancient tyrants made a practice of inflicting the most fiendish suffering upon their captured enemies, or in fact upon their most loyal underlings when the fancy happened to take them, for no reason other than the pleasure it gave them to observe extreme pain in others. In this same way, the chief of an uncivilized and particularly vicious tribe in some remote corner of the world might act, even today. To be completely fair, we must admit that Hitler was slightly above this sort of thing.

This brings me to the next point; a much more important one. The question—and it is the real crux of the matter—has to do with public opinion, past and present: how it is affected by the atrocities of tyrants, and also what effect it has on tyrants. In the operation of his extermination centers, Hitler went to great lengths to conceal what was taking place from his own people, and his reasons were, without doubt entirely pragmatic. Like all modern despots, Hitler went to great trouble in order to hide the worst of his excesses, not only from the eyes of the world, but also from his most ardent supporters. It surely cannot be considered with any seriousness that this was in any way due to a guilt complex by Hitler and his kind, as such a thing must be utterly foreign to such as these. Nor can we assume that cover-ups of this type are made because of consideration of the sensitivities of the public. The reason, then, must certainly be one of fear for their own positions. They are obviously, and probably for good reason, afraid of public opinion. This is, I maintain, the best obtainable answer which we have. We must look, not so much to the moralities of individual rulers here and there throughout history, as to the moral and ethical standards of the great mass of the ordinary people, and their effect—or lack of it—upon the rulers of their time. It is difficult to imagine one of the Pharaohs of ancient Egypt, for instance, being even slightly concerned about the feelings of his subjects at times when he had occasion to put to death several hundreds of his slaves for some slight or imagined dereliction of duty, or indeed for no reason at all other than his own amusement. In all probability, it is more likely that he would have been deemed to be an unfit ruler by his own people had he failed to do something like this at times when other forms of amusements were at a low ebb.

The greatest benefactors of mankind, those who have been in the main responsible for whatever improvement there has been in ethical standards, have been individuals acting somewhat in isolation. (When I speak of isolation I am referring to intellectual isolation, since most of them were, in this way, far ahead of their own followers.) Judging from readily available evidence, these men would appear to have had a much greater and more lasting effect on the rest of us than was the case with their amoral counterparts. (The latter category is quite apart from any of the out-and-out tyrants.) The names which come to mind most readily in this respect are those of Socrates, Jesus, Lincoln and Gandhi—to mention a very few of the topmost rank. By the very nature of things, it was inevitable that these men were all far in advance of their times; and, as a result of their great and good humanitarism, most of them were rewarded by being roundly condemned, ostracized, and even—especially in ancient times—put to death. The list of such people, including of course, both men and women, is extremely long and would no doubt run into many millions were we to include all who in some way have in the past made, or are now making a worthwhile contribution to the thinking of the world. As a Canadian, I am proud to mention the name of a fellow countryman of mine—one who must rank high on any such list, that of the late James S. Woodsworth.

Against the influence of these saint-like people there must be balanced a group, possibly smaller in numbers but infinitely more wealthy and powerful, and wielding a much greater immediate influence upon public opinion. I am not thinking here of the well known tyrants and despots, nor of the lesser known but equally infamous robbers, pirates and outlaws of history. These people were, almost without exception so entirely lacking in even the slightest decency that they unintentionally became horrible examples. In this way they inadvertently made sure that their influence was negative with respect to their moral standards. Those who I have in mind are more numerous, powerful and dangerous. They make a pretense of being benefactors of society when in fact their real motives are something entirely different. Their actual motivations are avaricious desires to exploit a stupid, lethargic and apathetic public; either of their own society or a more illiterate and helpless people elsewhere. Some individuals of this largely amoral group may actually do a great deal of good during their lifetimes, but with such as they, the good accomplished is always and inevitably more than offset, and usually much more than offset, by the impediment to human advancement which they create. Their chief means of doing evil is by the abuse, misuse and out-and-out prostitution of the means of mass public information, which at the present time consists mainly of the press, radio, T.V., and the motion pictures. (I have even seen this sort of rubbish sneaked into crossword puzzles.) Many names come quite easily to mind but a very few will suffice: Bismark, Zaharoff, Krupp, Chaing Kai-Shek, Vanderbilt, Northcott, Hearst, Beaverbrook, McCormick, Joseph McCarthy, Richard Nixon and Herbert Holt. (It may be of interest that the first draft of this chapter was written and this list complied some years prior to Nixon's election to the presidency of the U.S.)

Such amoral detriments of society have existed and have exercised immense power throughout all history, but despite all of their efforts, our ethical norms have continued to rise—slowly and unsteadily to be sure—but rise nevertheless. I can see no valid reason for it to be otherwise henceforth. In spite of all the wealth, power and influence of this group, their effect on human thought and behavior can never quite counteract that of those who possess greatly superior principles.

In attempting to outline my reasons for my contention that our ethical patterns are constantly improving, I have tried to compare, briefly, the worst elements of our race with the best. And, more importantly, I attempt a comparison of their lasting effect on our thinking. I attempt also, to judge our present standards of conduct against those of past ages. Before leaving the subject I propose making two more comparisons of a more specific nature.

The first of these is that of a man of some thirty centuries ago against his more or less exact present day counterpart. The individual I have in mind is Ulysses, who is portrayed as being a god-like man with the very highest of human attributes, and with the highest of reputations among his contemporaries. There is a likelihood that such a person never actually existed and that he was nothing more than a fictitious character created by Homer, who was possibly the first poet in history whose works have come down to us. I understand that Homer is believed to have lived during the ninth century, B.C. Whether Ulysses was at one time a real living man, or was merely a figment of Homer's imagination is, for my purposes at least, beside the point. In either case he was depicted quite seriously, and evidently accepted at that time as being the most just and noble of men, possessing all of the human virtues, plus a few godlike characteristics, with few or none of the usual vices or weaknesses; a paragon of incorruptible faultlessness, and a man esteemed, respected and admired by his own and succeeding generations.

I must stress that I am in no way attempting to pass judgment upon, or to criticize Homer as a writer, since I have no knowledge of the ancient Greek language. Whatever knowledge of his works that I possess has been gained through translations, and from the writings of others. My only real concern of him is in regard to his concept of the highest in moral conduct. It would seem from what I know of his works, especially *The Odyssey,* that the character of Ulysses which he described actually represented his conception of what in his time would have been regarded as just about the highest in human qualities. I can find no reason to doubt that the picture of this hero which I have gathered is reasonably close to the one which he intended to convey. There is no need for me to outline all of the activities of this supposedly noble character as set forth by Homer. Let me say, however, that I take the most serious objection to many of his actions as being entirely unfit for any person possessing a bare modicum of decency, let alone one of godlike attributes. One example alone of his conduct will serve to illustrate my point. Upon his return to Ithaca, after twenty years of war and wandering, including four or five years which he spent "shacked up" with a temporary girl friend, Calypso, he proceeded in a manner which amounted almost to murder, with the help of his son and several loyal underlings, to exterminate all of the suitors of Penelope, whom they had every right to regard as a widow. There was some justification for this action, since these men had been sponging upon and depleting his estate for a long number of years. I feel that my action would be about equal to his if I were to catch a group of young men in the act of siphoning gasoline from my automobile, and were to proceed to shoot every last one of them to death.

Following the disposition of the suitors, Ulysses, the great and godlike man that he was supposed to be, then displayed charity and merciful generosity by condescending to spare the lives of several of his former retainers who were able to prove their loyalty to him beyond any possible doubt. It was an entirely different matter with a group of possibly a dozen women who begged for their lives. These woman had the status of domestic servants and very little more. It would seem probable that most of them had never even seen Ulysses previously but had accepted the status quo as it existed. In any case, these women had, over a period of time accepted the suitors as their masters and had attended to their needs, perhaps in matters of sex as well as in other ways. Our noble hero, not wishing to take any hasty or ill-advised measures, ordered them to be held prisoners until the following day while he took the matter under advisement. After due deliberation, the just, great and good Ulysses appears to have taken much satisfaction in personally supervising the hanging of these unfortunate creatures.

This may have been Homer's conception of the ultimate in human greatness, but with all deference to his genius as a writer, I must dissent. In moral and ethical norms, I am inclined to classify him as being about equal to the late Al Capone. I simply cannot imagine a leading writer of this century producing a long epic extolling the virtues of the great, wonderful and god-like Mr. Capone.

The second of these comparisons which might prove to be worth a brief glance is that of Socrates against his modern counterparts, especially in respect to the way in which he was regarded by the general public of his day, as against his present day equivalent. Socrates was, of course, condemned and put to death for what in essence amounted to teaching the young to think for themselves, instead of blindly accepting the opinions of their more orthodox mentors. It would seem difficult to imagine any such punishment being meted out to, say, a present day instructor at university level for attempting the same thing. In this, I do not mean the teaching of exactly what Socrates taught; for, in addition to encouraging his students to think for themselves, it must be assumed that he held certain opinions which he must have, perhaps even unwittingly, passed on to them. The teacher with whom I wish to compare him is one who at present interests his students in philosophies which are considered to be as radical at this time in history, as were those of Socrates in his day. Such a teacher might well find himself out of employment, or at least might have to choose his school carefully, but it is difficult to imagine anything in the way of more severe chastisement being administered to him, even in that great neighbor of my country, the U.S.A.

Before proceeding further, I feel that I should make a few explanations in clarification of my opinions regarding this big and powerful nation. During the course of my discussions I will, on a few occasions, be disposed to make some rather critical comments about it. My purpose at this time is to ensure that these criticisms are to be, on no account, taken as a blanket condemnation of the entire nation and everything that it has done or is doing: nor must it be taken as a condemnation of all Americans. This is most definitely not my intention.

Judging from my own knowledge, I am quite sure that on an average, Americans are in no way inferior to Canadians, nor, for that matter, to any other peoples of the world. Every nation should be held accountable for its misdeeds, as is the case with every individual. And all countries in the world have much to account for. This certainly includes both Canada and the U.S. My excuse for pointing to those of the U.S. is that they serve better to illustrate my points for the reason that it is by far the most powerful and influential nation of the "Western World". Its misdeeds are most sharply in focus due to their nearness in time and distance. Also, for the last few decades it has taken upon itself the authority to shape the entire world in a manner dictated by its wealthy and powerful hierarchy. In this connection it is no more than fair to point out that, although Canada was not an active participant in most of these events, my country was, at least in most cases, a willing lackey.

When I speak of the wealthy and powerful minority of Americans, it should be understood that a fairly exact equivalent exists in Canada, and in fact may well have taken part in the misdeeds of the larger country. And I am convinced also, that it can be stated with confidence that about the same proportion of Canadians were taken in by American propaganda attempting to justify their evil actions, as was the case in the U.S. It is not too much to say that in almost every case they had our approval and support.

In view of all this, it is obvious that we Canadians must accept our full share of blame, and must surely not be so ill-advised as to consider ourselves in any way superior.

Several paragraphs back I had something to say concerning the modern counterpart of Socrates, and that in my opinion, he would be in no danger of facing severe punishment, to say nothing of the frightful penalty inflicted on Socrates. In stating this opinion I am entirely cognizant of the sad and lamentble fact that during my own time, no less than five people have been put to death in the U.S.A.—four by electrocution and one by a firing squad—for what was in actuality the holding and spreading of opinions widely divergent from those of the wealthy and influential minority.

It might be well, in passing, to mention a few of the circumstances of these accusations and convictions; and also the names of the victims of these atrocities. Three trials were involved and all three were prime examples of American jurisprudence at its very lowest ebb. The first was the trial of Joe Hill who was executed by a firing squad in 1915. Hill was one of the founders and exponents of the despised Industrial Workers of the World. I remember very well as a boy and as a young man, this organization being held by the general Public in the type of scorn and hatred usually reserved for the vilest of criminals. Their leaders, of whom Hill was one—and however mistaken they may have been in some of their views—were idealists who devoted their lives to what they believed to be a worthy cause. Hill was unlucky enough to have been someplace near the scene of a robbery and murder. This was sufficient evidence for the authorities and his execution followed a mock trial. Attempts during subsequent years have been made to clear his name but have come to naught as a result of all of the records of his trial having been unfortunately "lost!" No more need be said.

The second of these inversions of justice concerned two men; Nicola Sacco, a cobbler, and Bartolmeo Vanzetti, a fish peddlar. They were also members of a far left organization which was making a sincere, although possibly quite mistaken, effort to interest the public in a better type of society. They were accused of a murder which had taken place somewhere in their vicinity, and were condemned on evidence, the vital core of which can most charitably be described as idiotic. This "trial" took place in 1921 and they were finally put to death by electrocution in 1927.

The third of this series of atrocities occurred during the infamous era of senator Joseph McCarthy. Its victims were two people, a husband and wife, Julius and Ethel Rosenberg. The whole event was utterly preposterous in two ways. They were accused of giving atomic secrets to another nation during wartime. The joker here is that the country to which this information was supposed to have been supplied was, at the time, far from being an enemy of the U.S., in fact an active ally. The other imbecility about the case was the fact that in all the history of the development of atomic bombs only one secret was ever held by the U.S. This one secret was disclosed, not by any foreign agents (which the Rosenbergs most certainly were not) but by the president of the U.S. Harry S. Truman when he announced to the world that the first atomic bomb had been successfully exploded. Prior to that time the whole idea had been based upon an unproven theory. At no time had there ever been any secrets about the science and technical knowledge about atomic energy and its possible uses, and once this announcement had been made, any country with sufficient resources could make an atomic bomb. But this did not deter the courts, and the Rosenbergs, who had previously been slightly interested in communistic activities, were convicted without anything in the way of substantial evidence, and were, like Sacco and Vanzetti, put to death by electrocution in 1953.

To get back to the influential American minority to which I referred a few paragraphs ago; this same minority comes close, on occasion, to wielding absolute control of majority public opinion, and consequently of all public affairs, both governmental and judicial, up to and including the supreme court of that country, which sometimes appears to be rather pathetically misled. Numerous other equally innocent and only slightly less unfortunate people, of this same country, and for the same general reason, have served or are even now serving, viciously long prison terms imposed upon them for the same sort of "crimes". None of these people were, in fact, tried in court for the conduct which actually brought them into disfavor with their ruling masters, but always on some trumped-up charge—in each case so patently false as to approach the point of absurdity. They were invariably convicted by a corrupt judicial system, regardless of the fact that in each case the great preponderance of evidence not only quite failed to indicate any crime whatever, but actually proved—at least to any observer of impartiality and fair-mindedness—their complete innocence.

The reason these people found themselves at odds with the influential class was that the ideology which they espoused, or were supposed to have espoused, was thought to pose a threat to the very existence of the privileged and wealthy minority. Whether or not it actually did so to any real extent is doubtful in the extreme. At any rate a considerable number of the elite few appeared to hold that view; inasmuch as they were able to hold any rational opinion at all, amid their fright and consternation. This, incidentally, brings to mind a terse and witty remark made by some sagacious individual during the great depression of the 1930s: "There is none so prone to panic as a frightened optimist." After having relieved myself of the above remarks (and warn that more of the same will be forthcoming) let me stress that the U.S. is by no means the only country in which such occurrences take place, nor is it even anywhere close to being the worst offender.

In each of these five cases of record, mentioned above, and in which capital punishment was involved, the unfortunate scapegoats were the victims of the most vicious and ghastly of all crimes: that of legalized homicide on obviously false charges. In each case the perpetrators of these atrocities seem to have given way to utter panic and indulged in excesses which eventually and inevitably result in an effect quite the reverse of that which they had hoped for. Similar results accrued to those responsible for the death of Socrates, but in his case it took a much longer time.

The important point here is that Socrates was tried and convicted for what were considered by his enemies to be moral crimes. It was not deemed necessary to indulge in any subterfuge or trickery in order to deceive the public. The citizens of this ancient community apparently thought it quite fitting that one be put to death for such things. Socrates, or any other person of early history, who engaged in, or was believed to have engaged in, any activity which could possibly threaten the position of the privileged class of that time, would almost certainly have been executed for treason, or something of the sort, with the likelihood that there would have been little or no protest from any quarter. When we compare this procedure with all the rigmarole gone through, with enormous pains taken to assuage public opinion in these recent American atrocities, we find a remarkable difference. Had these people been tried openly on charges arising directly from the activities for which they were in fact convicted, the results would most certainly have been much different. The American public, had they been aware of the truth, would never have stood for any of these convictions. However, the great mass of them, being as easily misled and as gullible as they are, were fooled, or at least a sufficient number were fooled to the extent which made these convictions possible. Even as it was, the more intelligent and better informed Americans—a minority, of course—together with their counterparts throughout the whole civilized world protested with such conviction and vehemence that these executions brought a measure of disgrace down upon the U.S.A.

It seems to me that if this matter is studied carefully, the only conclusion possible is that mankind's moral and ethical standards have most definitely improved during recorded history. No reason is apparent why they should do otherwise henceforth, provided that the human race continues in existence. I would, in fact, predict that it will proceed upward at an accelerated rate corresponding to the upward course of health, longevity, intelligence, and skill.

It must not be assumed from these remarks that, in my opinion, we should congratulate ourselves, or be in any way complacent about the present state of our ethics. Indeed, I believe that they are quite deplorable, and that we have an enormous distance to travel before we achieve even a tolerable state of decency in respect to such standards. All that I have tried to show is that we have made slight but definite gains during our past history. As to the standards of any possible visitors from somewhere in remote space, all that we can learn from our own history would seem to indicate that their ethics would be higher than ours in about the same ratio as their intelligence would be above ours.

4 Intelligent Life Elsewhere in the Universe

In assessing the possibility of intelligent life in other parts of the cosmos we have one solid base from which to start: We are here now. Life on this planet clearly began as a result of one out of only two possible causes. Either life started spontaneously when the environment became suitable, or it was put here by some other intelligent life. In either case the final result is the same.

In the first case, assuming that we rose spontaneously, we must take it as a certainty that similar life has sprung up in other places, and without doubt, in an enormous number of other places. The lastest estimate, as far as I am aware, is that there are likely a million other planets such as our own, capable of bearing life as we know it, within our own galaxy; and the estimate of this number is constantly being revised upward. Since it is believed that there are one hundred billion stars within this galaxy, the figure of one million would seem to be rather on the conservative side. Estimates as to the number of galaxies within reach of present day radio telescopes, put the figure at about 600 billion. This would be within five or six billion light years. The number outside of this range must be quite beyond the scope of our imagination, and must be considered infinite. For these reasons, the odds that life exists somewhere other than on our planet would seem to be overwhelming, and must be taken to be a certainty. There can be no doubt that a very large number of civilizations have arisen and that others are constantly arising. In all probability, a relatively small number are somewhere close to our present state of development, an infinite number of others are an extremely long distance ahead of us, and a scattered few even slightly behind us. If we carry this logic a step further, it would seem from the conclusions I have reached that, during the eons of time past, an enormous number of these civilizations have reached the point of being all-knowing and all-powerful. They are at present what we in our semi-barbaric and superstitious state would call "godlike" in their wisdom and omnipotence. This state may have been arrived at by means somewhat along the lines I have suggested. It is entirely possible, on the other hand, that this position could have been reached in a manner which is quite impossible for me to understand. In any case I cannot come to any conclusion other than that a great many of them have arrived at this position in one way or another.

Regarding the second possibility, that this planet's life was put here deliberately, and in such a manner that we would evolve as we actually have done, then the assumption must be that whoever put us here had arisen to a position of eminence by means somewhat similar to those which I have suggested. It is apparent then, that the two roads converge at this point, and as far as we are concerned, it is of no importance whether we arose spontaneously or were put here by some other intelligence. As to the assertion that an enormous number of super-civilizations, so much superior to ours as to approach the infinite, have arisen, and that intelligences from some or many of them have an interest in us at present, there is at least a little discernable evidence to support this view. I intend to return to this assertion some pages further on in this discussion.

As recently as forty-odd years ago the opinion was held by some reputable scientists, and probably shared by most of their fellows, that the possibility of any life existing other than on this planet was so remote as to border on the fantastic. Those to whom I refer took an entirely materialistic approach to the matter as opposed to a religious approach. Religious leaders have always, as far as I am aware, held that this earth was the only part of all space—at least physical space—that counted for anything. In recent years, some religious thought may have been veering away from this concept, but to what extent I am unable to say; nor am I greatly concerned. In my early youth, I learned the complete futility of any attempt at an intelligent and objective discussion of anything even remotely pertaining to religion, with any person of more than slight conviction in that direction. The very fact that these people hold such nonsensical beliefs comprises in itself fairly substantial proof that they have been so thoroughly indoctrinated that they have ceased to use whatever powers of logic they may possess for anything except the most mundane purposes. To do otherwise would surely lead to an undermining of their comfortable head-in-the-sand retreat from reality.

It is not my contention that any more than a very small minority of those holding such beliefs are in any way evil. On the contrary, virtually all of the people of religious conviction whom I know, or have known, are or were almost entirely good. I contend merely that they are incapable of anything much in the way of logical abstractions on any subject having to do with religion. My remarks in pursuit of my nebulous philosophies are not for them but are addressed elsewhere. It is my intention to say a few words later in this discourse about religious beliefs and their effect on human thought throughout history. For the moment I will say only that my objections to religion generally may be largely summed up in one word: faith. Any concept which, if accepted at all, must be taken on nothing more than blind, ignorant and unreasoning faith, must of necessity be completelely bankrupt. This is manifestly the case with the vital core of all religion.

Some thirty years ago, a small book entitled "The Final

Judgment" emerged from the pen of the late J.B.S. Haldane. This man was a noted biologist whose knowledge extended in no small way into other scientific realms. He was, and still is held in high esteem by the educated world. I read this little book as a young man in the early 1930s, and to say that I was greatly impressed would be something of an understatement. But in spite of my admiration for Mr. Haldane, I found myself in sharp disagreement with him in connection with two of his conclusions, one explicitly stated and the other implied by what he said.

The first and explicit conclusion was his assertion of the above-mentioned theory that life almost certainly existed nowhere else than on this planet. His arguments leading to this deduction accepted without reservation the theory that the planets of our little solar system were originally formed by small fragments broken from our sun, possibly due to a particularly severe explosion. As he points out, the relationship of the planets to the sun should, by all known laws of physics, have been similar to that of our moon to the earth. This would have obviously resulted in a condition making the kind of life with which we are familiar virtually impossible. (He did not in fact go so far as to make this qualification but seemed to suggest that life as found on our earth is the only possible sort.) He concluded that this condition must have materialized due to totally unexplained causes of such unusual nature as to make the resulting condition absolutely unique throughout the entire length and breadth of the universe. As a matter of fact, several other theories have been advanced as to the formation of our planetary system. I understand that some of these had been put forward prior to Haldane's writing of this book, and I cannot think that he was unfamiliar with them; but for some reason he appears to have rejected all but the one mentioned above.

I found that I could not accept this conclusion at the time when I first read this book. I still cannot: the ensuing years have served only to strengthen my objections, which I'll attempt to outline as briefly as possible

The first of these reasons I have already hinted at, but I would like to underscore my thoughts on the matter by use of an illustrating parallel. Imagine a man living in almost complete isolation from the main stream of society: a man of considerable natural intelligence and highly cultured within the limits imposed by his circumstances. Let us suppose that he is, for instance, an Arab living with only his own kind somewhere near the center of the Sahara Desert, and who has never seen or heard of any of the world's oceans, rivers or lakes, nor any body of water larger than a pool which might be found at a desert oasis. Upon hearing rumours of marine life existing entirely below water, his reaction might well be about the same as that implied by Mr. Haldane: "That this story is fallacious must be quite obvious to all. It is common knowledge that life simply cannot be sustained under water for more than a very short time. I myself have seen both men and animals perish from being kept below water for no more than ten minutes. The supposition is quite preposterous."
supposition is quite preposterous."

My second reason has to do with probability. Assuming that our solar system was actually formed in the manner outlined by Haldane, is it possible that the circumstances were as completely unique as he suggests? I would have to guess that the answer is most definitely in the negative. If certain causes result in one very peculiar and unlikely effect due to unusual circumstances on one occasion, then surely the same effect will turn up again, provided that there is a sufficiently large number of opportunities. When we consider the millions of planetary systems which are thought to exist within our galaxy, and the number of known galaxies—something in the order of 600 billion—and that only a tiny fraction, in all probability, of the total, then it would appear that in total the opportunities must closely approach an infinite number. We must then conclude that what seemed to be no more than a remote chance has become a virtual certainty.

Third and last, is the explanation itself of the manner in which our solar system was formed. Haldane seems to have accepted without question the traditional and long accepted theory that our world and the other planets are the result of fragments broken from our sun. If this theory required something like several hundreds of millions to one odds to obtain the results actually achieved, then it would seem to me that we would be well advised to exhaust all other possibilities in an effort to find a more plausible explanation before this one is accepted. Just what, if any, theories of a more reasonable nature might be available, I had not the slightest notion at the time.

Since then the answer has come to light most clearly. It appeared in another small but—to my way of thinking—most important book. This book is entitled "The Nature of the Universe", written by another eminent scientist, Fred Hoyle, and was published in 1950. In this book Hoyle suggests that our planetary system did not spring originally from the sun. According to the theory espoused by Hoyle, but which may not have originated with him, our planets were formed out of relatively small fragments left from the disintegration of a star which had previously been a twin to our sun. It is unnecessary for me to point out that this explanation is much more feasible than the other. Hoyle estimated, when he wrote this book, that within our galaxy there are some ten thousand planets whose similarity to our earth is such as to allow them to support life in the form with which we are familiar. Since that time, this estimate has been revised upward considerably by other experts on the subject, (and I do not doubt that Hoyle agrees with them) and now stands at several millions.

The second point about which I found myself in disagreement with Haldane concerns his implied assertion that our knowledge of science, and other matters, had just about reached its final state and that all which remained to be done were a few relatively minor refinements and applications of principles already understood; and that in all other respects we had gone about as far as we ever could. He intimated that the answers to a whole multitude of questions facing us at present would remain forever a mystery. He seemed to assume, for instance, that we would never be able to understand or to control gravity. Personally, I am inclined to take it to be nothing less than a certainty that this force, which is as yet so completely puzzling and unexplainable, will be altogether understood and controllable at some future time. As to when this breakthrough might occur I have no idea, as I have never pretended to anything much more than the average layman's knowledge of any subject pertaining to science. This event may come upon us rather soon, and even be an accepted fact by the advent of the twenty-first century, just as our blundering but more or less successful attempts at space travel are accepted today. I would have to think that it is more likely centuries than decades away; but it is obviously apparent that it must come prior to the time when our efforts at space travel advance much beyond their present swaddling clothes state. That is, before any attempts at interstellar travel are made.

As another example of the same disagreement, Haldane appeared to accept as a certainty the opinion that the human life span would never be greatly extended beyond its present length. It seems self-evident to me that in time—always provided that the human race survives—our life span will continue to increase until, during the course of many centures, it approaches the state of being unlimited.

Following this line of reasoning, the inevitable conclusion would appear to be that intelligent life exists at many other places throughout the cosmos. The number of such places must be very large, and, with our lack of ability to comprehend matters of this kind, we must consider it to be infinite. However, for purposes of this discussion I find it necessary to deem it to be finite, for the reason that any conception of a fraction of an unlimited number is beyond my capability. With the ground rules in this way somewhat established, and the conclusion of other intelligent life accepted, then the question naturally arises concerning the present state of advancement of these civilizations. Many people might ask: have any of them reached our great state of advancement? I prefer to turn the question around and ask whether any of them could possibly have remained in our deplorable state of retardation. Actually, the probability is that we are somewhere in the lowest range. This assertion may seem to be unwarranted, and nothing much more than a guess. My contention stems from the unquestioned fact that our progress has, for the most part, been attained within the past two or three centuries; that although man has been capable of serious and wise thoughts—at least in certain individual cases—for the past three or four millenniums, there is no evidence that such was the case much prior to that time. Here the assumption must be that when wise and intelligent life exists, ways are found of recording the thoughts of such life. In any case, life in its most primitive form has existed on this planet for no more than some forty million years, and it would seem to require that much time for a super-civilization to show the first signs of emerging.

To me, it would appear absurd to deny the virtual certainty that other intelligent life was at about our present state at the time when life here first began. This is likely the case in a great many places scattered throughout the cosmos. An enormous number of others probably originated at a much earlier time, with a large number having, long before the present time, reached a degree of development quite beyond our conception. Still others may have arrived later; a few even later than ourselves, while still others will be constantly arising as time goes on. It is with the most advanced of these groups that I am concerned. Any conclusions which we reach regarding our ultimate attainments would, of course, apply to them. Because we can assume that these goals are limited only by physical possibilities, it is entirely safe to say that the most advanced of these groups must long ago have reached a close approximation to the ultimate with respect to their standards of ethics, intelligence and intellect, and also with their accomplishments. To me, this state of affairs would seem to be a certainty.

At this point I propose to take up a matter which, although it may be of some interest, will, I feel sure, in the final analysis prove to be no more than academic, as I will try to show in this discourse. This is the question as to whether the cosmos might be described as being in a constant state as opposed to its having been formed—or possibly more correctly—reformed—by a super-gigantic explosion some thirteen billion years ago. At first glance this would appear to be an absurd point about which to quibble. Judged within our terms of references, that length of time could be considered infinite, but this is not the case when viewed from a larger perspective.

I have been quite interested in this more or less current theory since its inception. However, it is my understanding that it may now be getting near to the point of being discarded. The theory to which I refer was espoused by almost all astronomers and cosmologists until a few years ago, and indeed, it may well be that most of them still cling to it at the present time. It resulted from the discovery of the now famous red shift observed in light from far distant sources. It was first observed by the eminent astronomer, William Hubble. The conclusion reached by Hubble, and concurred with by other important and learned men in his field, was that, where this red shift was observed it indicated that the galaxy from which the light emanated was moving away from us at a high rate of speed, and that this rate of speed was directly proportional to the distance separating the observed galaxy from us. Judging from such information as I have been able to gather on the subject, I have to say that this conclusion is open to some question. I say this despite my great admiration for these men and their accomplishments. As is the case with many other people whose great knowledge is confined to narrow fields, they have the tendency of being unable to see the forest for trees.

The theory of the great explosion which is supposed to

have caused the creation of all of the known galaxies is thought to have something of a parallel with a particle of gas released—and consequently exploding—in a perfect vacuum of great size and out of the influence of all fields of gravitation. In this case, each molecule of the substance comprising this particle, begins moving away from every other molecule at various rates of speed depending on their respective locations within the gas particle at the time of the explosion. They have presumably been shown to move away from each other at a constant rate of speed. This divergent movement should, according to theory, continue ad infinitum provided that their field is unlimited. The difficulty with this theory is that the movement of these molecules should eventually be overcome by their mutual gravity, and they should begin to come together again, and in time form another cohesive mass.

It is possible that some procedure of the same sort may be true of the galaxies of which we have any knowledge, and that in the course of time—probably something in the order of 30 billion years—they may once again come together in a great mass. By this means, the stage could be set for another super-explosion. This theory must be judged on whatever evidence is available at present, until such time as more becomes available.

An objection to the big explosion theory has to do with the number of galaxies visible to us when we look out into space in every direction. We must assume that any such explosion involves, not the entire cosmos, but only a relatively small portion of the infinite whole. If this is the case, and provided that our earth is not close to the exact center of the explosion—which would seem to be extremely unlikely—then the supposition must be that, in looking out in various directions, the number of galaxies visible would be at a maximum in one direction and at a minimum in the opposite direction, and that the difference would in all likelihood be quite noticeable. This is, I understand, not the case: the number is equal in any direction we care to look.

At present the supporting evidence for the big explosion theory is that of the Doppler effect of light observed from distant sources. This, in almost every case, seems to indicate a shift toward the red side of the spectrum, or, which is the same thing, a slowing down of the frequency of the light waves. The first, and by far the most obvious explanation for this shift, is that the source of this particular light is (or was) moving away from us. Very roughly, the indicated speed of recession of the light sources outside of our own galaxy is as follows.

There are 23 galaxies located within 2.5 million light years of us. I understand that these are too close for their light to have any spectrum shift which is measurable by any means we have at present.

Galaxies located 50 million light years distant appear to be receding at 750 miles per second.

Galaxies located 650 million light years distant appear to be receding at 9300 miles per second.

Galaxies located 940 million light years distant appear to be receding at 13,400 miles per second.

Galaxies located 1.7 billion light years distant appear to be receding at 24400 miles per second.

Galaxies located 2.7 billion light years distant appear to be receding at 38000 miles per second.

Galaxies located 4.0 billion light years distant appear to be receding at 124000 miles per second or about 2/3 the speed of light.

Galaxies barely discernible by visible means and possibly 5 billion light years distant are thought to be receding at about 3/4 the speed of light.

Galaxies at the outer limits discernible by radio telescopes are thought to be receding at something in the order of 9/10 the speed of light.

At this point the big explosion theory begins to look slightly ridiculous.

Some years ago, possibly during the early 1960s, I read an article concerning this matter which outlined an alternate theory. I do not know who originated this theory, or whether it ever gained any favor in the scientific world, but it impressed me greatly. This theory, to state it as briefly as possible, suggested that the red shift indicated merely that the frequency of the light rays was slowing down as a result of an aging process. This would obviously result in a shift toward the red side of the spectrum. The light in which this shift is observed has been travelling through space for a period of up to five billion years, and it would seem reasonable that it should be constantly transforming an infinitesimal amount of its energy into matter. This would eventually cause a diminution to an extent that light would, during the course of billions of years, be completely transformed into matter. The postulation here was that this could account for the masses of dust—supposed in some quarters to be made up of hydrogen atoms—which are thought to form clouds throughout all observable space.

It is a great deal easier for me to accept this theory than it is for me to believe that all of the more distant galaxies about which we have knowledge, are racing away from us and from each other at speeds which in some cases approach the speed of light.

If this proposition is carried a step further it could account for the formation of new galaxies. It is, I understand, generally agreed that new galaxies are constantly being formed; that they mature, grow old and eventually die during eons of time.

After making the above assertion with respect to galaxies, I wish to state my convictions regarding the relationship and interchangeability of light—or any radiated, or other type of energy—and mass. I assume that any kind of energy can be changed into any other kind of energy; that matter can be changed into any other kind of matter; that either can be transformed into the other; but that it is impossible for either to be destroyed. I believe that these assertions are accepted at present, in a general sort of way, by the scientific world. At the same time there are, no doubt, many knowledgeable people who have serious misgivings about human ability to ever accomplish any such transformations. I am convinced that we will eventually gain the necessary skill to make these transformations, given sufficient time, intelligence and effort.

It is evident that any galaxy, from the time of its beginning must lose more energy through radiation than it gains, which is confirmed by the clouds of atoms. This process of radiation of energy, either within the light spectrum or otherwise, would continue as long as sufficient heat remains. In this way an aging galaxy would either be entirely consumed or, more likely continue to float around in space until it is swept up with an enormous mass of free atoms in the formation of a new galaxy. Radiated energy would continue through space until either it strikes some object and is transformed into heat, or continues for five or six billion years, at which time it becomes some kind of matter, possibly hydrogen atoms. In this way a continuous cycle is maintained.

I must emphasize that I am most definitely not attempting to rule out the large explosion theory. For one such as myself to do so would be nothing less than presumptuous. Such a theory may possibly be the correct one. I am stating merely that to me the aging light theory is much more attractive and more likely to be proven, eventually, to be the right one. If, however, the explosion theory is indeed correct, we must assume that over a period of something like 30 billion years a large number of galaxies (that is, large by our standards) are drawn together by mutual gravitation to form an enormous mass which, when large enough, results in an explosive situation. The so-called "Big Bang" then takes place and another cycle is begun. This event would presumably be repeated every thirty or so billion years. I would be most hesitant, however, to suggest that the entire universe is involved in any such event. I cannot envisage the cosmos as being anything other than infinite, which would make such an explosion impossible. Should such upheavals occur periodically, I would think it more likely that they involve only a comparatively small part of the infinite whole. It is obvious that any part of the cosmos, must of necessity be an infinitely small portion. If this assumption is correct, then it would seem that explosions of this kind are occurring constantly throughout all space.

When we consider the speed at which the more distant galaxies about which we have knowledge appear to be receding from us, sometimes reaching almost the speed of light, then this theory appears to be—at least to a non-expert in such matters—slightly absurd. Juding from what information I have been able to gather on the subject, I am inclined to favor the alternate choice as being more attractive and more probable. In saying this I am not disputing the reality of the Doppler effect. My assertion is nothing more than that it is not the only possible cause of a red shift. There are at least one or two cases where a blue shift has been noted. It would be difficult to attribute a shift in this direction to any cause other than that the source of light is moving in our direction. Assuming that the explosion hypothesis is a fallacy, there are, no doubt, instances where the red shift is due, at least in part, to the movement of the light source away from us.

A matter which comes naturally to mind in a discussion of this type is that of the theories of Einstein. These theories, if my rudimentary understanding of them is correct, hold that all space is curved; that light travels in a slight continuous arc; that mass changes its form when moving at extremely high rates of speed; and that time slows down—or has the effect of slowing down—as speed increases. It is surely not for me to either dispute or support these theories. It is enough for me to say that I am an admirer of this great scientist and philosopher. However, I may perhaps be permitted to make a few observations concerning his philosopies without in any way attempting to add to or detract from his great intellectual stature.

One of the books on the subject attempted to explain some

of these theories but, in my estimation did not do too well or go very far in this direction. It could be that the fault was entirely mine and due solely to my ignorance. The author of this book went to great lengths in several rather long chapters in an effort to explain how space is curved, giving a number of illustrations in an attempt to make it clear. After completing all of his lengthy explanations, he ended with the remark, "Of course, outside all of this there must be something else." In my opinion, this completely negated all of his arguments.

A few years ago I read of a great discovery by an eminent astronomer, which was acclaimed as giving truth to Einstein's theory regarding light travelling through space in a slight arc. This astronomer had observed light from a star which was at the time known to be behind the sun. I gather from what I read that this was supposed to be proof positive that light rays do in fact travel in an arc. To my way of thinking, it proved only that light rays can be made to bend, as apparently was the case when these particular rays passed close to the sun. To me, this would seem to indicate nothing more than the fact that light rays have mass. I believe that the theory of light rays having mass has been fairly well established. Light rays may actually bend slightly and continuously in the course of their long journey through space, but I contend that this astronomer did nothing whatever on that particular occasion to prove that contention.

Some time ago, I was considering this matter while standing near a bank of the Fraser River near the town of Hope in British Columbia. At this place the river makes a gradual and sweeping bend to my right at the point where I stood. I imagined my visibility to be limited to about one half mile in any direction and wondered what my thoughts would have been supposing that I had no knowledge of the Fraser, or of any kind of moving bodies of water. It occurred to me that upon seeing the water of this river bend slightly to my right, I may well have reached the conclusion, which could have been considered to be not unreasonable, that all rivers flow in a continuous clockwise circle. There may have been a slight similarity between this supposed deduction of mine and that of the astronomer mentioned above.

An eminent scientist and an authority on the subject made the assertion not so very many years ago that of the two theories regarding the transmission of light through empty space, the wave theory was impossible and the mass theory was incomprehensible. While he was obviously quite correct in his assessment of the wave theory, I would most humbly suggest that the mass theory is not quite as obscure as he indicated. It has, I believe, been fairly well substantiated—possibly subsequently to his making this remark—that light rays do consist of small particles of matter which are emitted under certain circumstances. The characteristics of these rays depend upon the substance from which they are emitted and the temperature of the substance at the time of their emission. They proceed in a stream, provided that the circumstances of their emission remain unaltered. These particles do not travel in a straight line but in a manner somewhat similar to a sine curve. This is, of course, quite apart from the slight curvature in their path suggested by Einstein. These light particles vibrate on sine waves of various frequencies which form the different colors.

While we do seem to have a sort of viable theory as to the make-up of light, we still have none at all regarding gravity, the nature of which remains, up to the present, a complete mystery. I understand that Einstein spent a good part of his life attempting to establish some sort of relationship among light, gravity and electro-magnetic waves. It would seem to be entirely likely that some such relationship exists, but Einstein appears to have had very little success in this part of his work. After all, his accomplishments were nothing less than monumental and he surely cannot be deprecated for his failure to bring this particular project to fruition.

On reading a book by Bertrand Russell, I was greatly interested in what he had to say in a section about Einstein and his works. Russell said that Einstein's observations in connection with problems which he was attempting to solve, were of a subjective nature. While his theories satisfied conditions as observed from our earth, the impression which I received from Russell was that these theories may well have been slightly different had he viewed the problems from a great many other points of up to perhaps two or three billion light years distant, and done so on a simultaneous basis. The lesson to be learned here is that when considering matters of a cosmic or of an inter-galaxial nature, they should be viewed in the widest possible perspective.

It may seem from my remakrs that I am attempting to set myself up as an authority on such subjects as astronomy and cosmology, among others, and with knowledge greater than that of the recognized experts in these fields. These foregoing remarks are not intended to leave any such impression, as I acknowledge these experts as my superiors and bow to their vast information in each of their fields. Before proceeding any further, I wish to make it clear as to just where I consider myself to be, in regard to knowledge and specialized learning. My formal education was small and sporadic, and in consequence, most of the knowledge which I have gathered has been the result of my own unorganized efforts. It has been the outcome of my reading, over a rather long period of years, on subjects which interest me (which have been many) with special emphasis on those which I attempt to deal with in this work. In this way I have acquired a veneer of learning covering a rather large area, but never much more than rather shallow anywhere. In all fairness I have to say that my present state of education, if judged by our usual standards, could best be described as mediocre.

There are occasions, it seems to me, when this state of knowledge (and lack thereof) is advantageous, and where a great deal of particularized knowledge, in some rare cases, is an encumbrance. This brings to mind a conversation which I had a number of years ago with a man who is well educated and a professional chemist, and as such, is doing good and useful work. This man's name is Elvins Spencer. He is, incidentally, the son of the late Henry Spencer, who was a noted political figure in the province of Alberta. Henry Spencer was a member of the Canadian Parliament from 921 until 1935.

During the conversation with Elvins Spencer, I made the remark that in my opinion, the future advances in chemistry might be more accurately judged by one not too well versed in the subject. As might be expected by those who know him well, he took what those who do not know him so well might have considered a surprisingly moderate attitude. I realized immediately that my utterance must have sounded quite idiotic to him, and that he would have been justified had he turned away after having given me a sharp retort. He neither did nor said anything of the kind, but replied politely that he felt the opposite to be true, and that the more a person knew about any subject the better he would be able to understand the possibilities for its advancement. I was about to pursue the matter further and try to explain that we were talking about two different things, but I decided that under the circumstances, and without a long and difficult discourse, it would be futile; so I decided to let the matter drop. What I might have said to him was that, of course he was right as far as the comparatively short range was concerned; that he was probably thinking in terms of a few decades at most while I was interested in trying to look ahead several millenniums at least. I quite believe that in this, there is something to be said for my point of view.

Before leaving the subject I would like to say now, and say quite categorically, that any and all developments which are being made now, and which will be made in the future by and for the human race, will be made by the Elvins Spencers of this world, and not by the Jack Turners.

This does not, however, rule out the possibility that those in my category might still be of some slight use. If we consider, for instance, the case of a sailing ship of several centuries ago attempting to sail into the north-west passage, trying to get through narrow and difficult channels, while avoiding enormous ice floes, I think we can find a rough parallel to what I am trying to show. In the case of this ship, the man who would be positioned at the topmost vantage point would be, I would think, surely not the best navigator nor the best seaman of the ship's company; certainly not the captain nor any of his senior officers, but an ordinary seaman, possibly without knowledge or ability in the operation of sailing ships, but one with no more qualifications than good eyesight and a fair amount of sound judgment. His job would be merely to point out channels which might seem to offer the best openings at places visible to him, but not to those on the deck of the ship. Those with greater skills would be occupied in attempting to manipulate the ship through these tricky and uncertain channels. In this particular case, there is clearly no reason why one of the expert seamen, possibly the captain himself, might not occasionally go up to the crow's nest to survey the situation. In circumstances of this kind an expert can easily take either a long or a short range view as he may choose, by nothing more than a change in his physical position. This parallel is illustrative only if the positions of the expert on the deck and the non-expert in the crow's nest are irreversible, with each permanently stationed.

When the example in the above situation is transferred to the field of scientific research in any of its multitude of branches, it may become a little clearer. The expert simply cannot transfer his position for the exact reason that he is an expert. He is unreservedly involved in the immediate problems and difficulties which must be overcome in order to achieve even a slight advancement; slight, that is, when viewed in the perspective of the ultimate, but enormous to those whose chief aim in life is to make it become a reality. It would be altogether too much to expect a research expert to divest himself of his vast amount of intimate knowledge and immediate concern of the project at hand, which he must do before climbing to a high vantage point for a long range view. This, at least, is the only conclusion which I am able to entertain with the help of whatever I have been able to learn during my lifetime.

5 What We Can Expect of the Future

For some years now science has been occupied with devising and putting into use a means of space travel. This space vehicle in its present form can hope to go not much farther than the confines of our little solar system. Only a few years ago, the first living foot stepped on our moon. This was considered a notable achievement, and rightly so. It is to me slightly ironic—but not at all surprising—that this great advancement was made by a country which, as I have tried to show, is rather lacking in ethical principles—at least in some areas. Such incongruities have been apparent throughout all history, and I suppose they will continue for some time yet. But in order to be fair, we must give this country all due credit for its achievements, as well as censure for its wrongdoings.

The opinion has been stated, and no doubt concurred in by those in the forefront of this great venture, that space travel can be possible only to a limited extent, and that any travel much beyond our solar system would seem to be quite out of the question for all time. The reasons stated for this impossibility are the limitations in the amount of mass which can be carried compared to the amount required for the propulsion of such an awkward vehicle for any significant distance beyond our planets; and also the shortness of the human life span. It is my firm conviction that both of these barriers, while entirely insurmountable for some considerable time in the future, will be overcome during the course of coming centuries. As soon as the nature of gravity is understood and this force becomes controllable, it is evident that with the advancement of atomic energy, the first of these problems can be defeated and, in so far as the vehicles are concerned, space travel can be made virtually limitless. As to the limits imposed by the human life span, I am convinced that this also will eventually be invalidated in two ways. In the first place, the type of craft used for interstellar travel could be vastly different and immensely larger than those used at present. They would have the obvious and tremendous advantage of being able to get out of our gravitational field with the expenditure of only the tiny amount of mass which would be needed for energy to overcome the earth's gravity. (It is possible that even this cost of energy could be made largely unnecessary by use of earth based devices.) Under these circumstances, instead of a few individuals, they could carry a whole colony of people living practically normal lives. With the establishment of artificial gravity, they would not have to contend with a weightless condition. As to the second method by which this difficulty could, and probably will, be overcome, I deem it to be nothing less than a certainty that human life will eventually be extended to a point where it becomes limitless.

There is also the speed factor to be considered. These same scientists, mentioned earlier in this text, seemed to be of the opinion that the rate of speed of the present vehicles is now at or near the maximum ever attainable. To me it appears quite obvious that such is by no means the case. With the control of gravity at our disposal, it is reasonable to assume that the speed of something in the order of 90 per cent of the speed of light may very well be attainable, and would be adequate to get us around within our galaxy in a reasonable amount of time. By this, I mean reasonable within the terms of reference which I have attempted to outline. It would be quite useless to venture upon any such travel as matters stand at present, or are likely to be within possibly the next several centuries, even provided that such speeds were attainable.

If my conclusions up to this point are accepted as being more or less correct, then it can be quite easily imagined that in the course of future millenniums—possibly a great many—the human race of which we are a part can eventually become the master of its own fate. With constantly increasing knowledge and intelligence, together with limitless life, we should be able to take complete control of galaxial matters. This statement is based on the utterly preposterous (and even idiotic) assumption that there is no other intelligent life within this galaxy. There is at present, of course, no proof that any other life exists, but the odds in its favor must be something much more than overwhelming. When the time comes we will, quite naturally, work in complete cooperation with other civilizations—most, if not all, of whom will be far in advance of us.

Some pages back I discussed the probability of a more or less continual cycle of galaxies being formed, coming to maturity and eventually dying over a period of a great many billions of years, as against that of a large number of galaxies being destroyed by coming together, and the resulting superexplosion with its inevitable catastrophic effects. As stated previously, I feel that I have substantial reasons for supporting the former theory. This whole question may seem to be somewhat academic in view of the fact that our solar system has an estimated five billion years to survive before our sun flares up in an immense burst of heat, which would be the beginning of its process of dying. After this difficulty has been overcome, and provided that the explosion theory is correct, there will be a longer interval before our galaxy expires. The gist of the matter here is that, while getting ourselves safely away from a dying sun to a more suitable location within our galaxy is no simple undertaking, still, the interval of five billion years should be ample time to prepare for such a trip. After a further lapse of possibly 15 billion years our galaxy would be in a state of decline, making an immensely more serious and difficult move necessary. At this time it would be necessary to leave, not only our galaxy, but the entire group destined to be part of the next great explosion. The problems involved in this kind of a manoeuvre would indeed be tremendous, but should not prove to be impossible. Again it is a case of virtually unlimited intelligence and resources being brought to bear on a problem which is not incapable of solution. It is for this reason I say that the question of the life cycle of galaxies is really not much more than academic.

Long before the period of five billion years has passed, and I would think not much more than a few millenniums into the future, several basic steps forward will have to be accomplished prior to anything more of importance being undertaken. Two of these I have already mentioned. One of them is the solution of the problem of gravity, which I do not propose to belabor any further here. Also, there is the matter which we are just now beginning to approach, that of being able to convert mass to energy and vice versa, as well as being able to convert any kind of mass to any other kind of mass. This brings to mind the old saw about the impossibility of making a silk purse out of a sow's ear. This will, no doubt come to be quite easily accomplished before a great deal more time has passed, although I most sincerely hope that when this time arrives we will have long since ceased treating animals in this ghastly manner. The conversion of mass and energy would seem to present no tremendous problems, and I would think that it and related questions should be entirely solved within the next few centuries. Another important subject is that of the production of synthetic food, but since this is no more than a segment of the previous question, the solutions should be arrived at simultaneously. The final topic of those which I wish to discuss now is that of the refinements to all of our planets and satellites, made in such a manner as to render them capable of sustaining life in an environment identical with, or similar to that of this earth. This could present a few problems.

Of all of the planets and satellites, our moon is obviously the first upon which this conversion might be carried out. Let me outline some of the steps which, in my judgment, might be taken to make the moon inhabitable by humans. I must assume that by this time, moon landings will have become commonplace with many people living there at selected spots and in shelters, on at least a semi-permanent basis. From this starting point three important steps would have to be taken. First, the gravity of the moon would have to be increased up to a value equal to that of the earth's, and controlled in such a way that its field does not extend more than a few hundred miles from its surface; otherwise it would, of course, affect the moon's orbit. Second, an adequate rotation would have to be established on the most suitable axis; and, third, an atmosphere very similar to ours would be needed and would have to be manufactured. This, obviously, could be made from whatever material was readily available. The increase in gravity would insure against the atmosphere floating away. The final process would be the transformation of the moon's surface to that similar to ours; with water, soil and vegetation. These would be required only to create a more pleasant environment, but not at all required to provide food. Methods of producing food synthetically will have been perfected long before technology has advanced sufficiently to make this conversion of the moon possible.

If this transformation of the moon is successful—and I have no doubt that this will be the case, by means somewhat as I have suggested or otherwise, then similar methods can be employed for the conversion of other planets and satellites. In some cases, particularly with the larger planets, the difficulties will, in all probability prove to be much greater.

For the purposes of this discussion I must assume that our race will be finding its way through all of these obstacles without any outside assistance whatever for a period of some hundreds of billions of years. I tried to explain previously my reasons for taking this utterly false supposition. And I will return to it again later.

Following this assumption, it is clear that it would be necessary for us to be continuously considering our future moves for as far ahead we are able to foresee. After the successful colonization of all our planets and satellites, the next major move would have to be that of getting away from our dying sun. This event should begin some five billion years hence. Regarding this long period of years, I would like to mention that, in the opinion of most people, this period of time is about the same as eternity, which is a rather shallow and thoughtless impression. If these same people, or at least the more intelligent of them were to think the matter out carefully, they would realize that time is, like space, in the final analysis only comparative and that a period such as five billion years is only a brief instant in comparison with all time. This should be obvious to any person with a modicum of intelligence who has given the subject any serious thought. I would like to interject here that in my experience most people, even the brightest, have a tendency to shy away from any contemplation of large amounts of time or distance. It is for this reason that they cannot, or at least do not, distinguish any difference between say, five billion years and five trillion years.

Possibly one of the more critical periods of this entire five billion years might be the next few decades—the time between the present and the middle of the next century. I realize, in saying this that I may be guilty of a mistake which I pointed out previously—that of taking a short-range view, and of failing to look at the situation in its proper perspective. In my suggestion regarding the next few decades I may be quite in error, but however that may be, I still must guess that if our race is able to survive the time I have mentioned, we should be good for at least quite a number of millenniums into the future. I must remind myself, though, that there are a great number of tremendous difficulties which will have to be overcome following the middle of the next century, most of which I cannot possibly foresee. I therefore must guard against advancing too vigorously a viewpoint which may be badly distorted. On the other hand, I must pursue the topic under discussion to my conclusions with all of the honesty and objectivity of which I am capable, and without falling into the even worse error of saying nothing at all for fear of mistakes.

Of all the problems confronting the human race at the present time, the foremost is merely the preservation of the race and the maintenance of its slow progress. One of the main and vital parts of this problem is that of human health and longevity. During the next few millenniums, if we are able to continue with something like our present rate of progress, we should be able to sustain human life at its maximum health and vigor for extremely long periods of time. Eventually, and long before five billion years have passed, human life should have become infinite. From the present day until this goal has been reached, this is, I suggest, a matter of the absolutely highest priority.

With the passing of the five billion years between the present time and the beginning of the dying process of our sun, and provided that all difficulties are successfully overcome, humanity should be able to avert the catastrophe which would otherwise have resulted. The most practical way of achieving this end, which I am able to visualize at this time would be the removal of all of the planets of our solar system away from our sun, to an environment where we could continue as planets around another sun which would have a good life expectancy. Judging by our standards this new star would be a considerable distance away. For instance, the nearest star to us is located about 4.3 light years distant. This is a very close neighbor within our galaxy. As a matter of comparison, our galaxy is disc-shaped and about 100,000 light years in diameter by about 15,000 light years thick. Incidentally the next nearest star is approximately 11 light years distant.

All of this means that, in the event that this journey is undertaken, the nearest star, Alpha Centauri, could possibly be reached in something under 10 years, provided that a speed of half of that of light could be attained. I am personally of the opinion that such an attainment is possible, if satisfactory progress is maintained during the intervening years. Should this be the case, then the most obvious difficulty would be that of providing something to take the place of the sun during this journey through space of relatively short duration. It is possible that the time required may be much greater than my estimate, since the speed which I mention may be found to be impracticable.

I do not see any reason for the impossibility of providing an artificial sun for this period of time, nor, as a matter of fact, for an enormously longer period. With the planets travelling in a fairly close group, a source of light of only a small fraction of the size of the sun, and in much closer proximity to the planets, should prove sufficient. This artificial sun would be expected to provide only light, as heat would be generated more economically from sources on each planet. The light from this little sun could be aimed to the places where it is required instead of being dissipated in all directions. At the same time it could be designed in such a way as to confine most of its radiation to the light segment of the spectrum.

Under these conditions, the limiting factor would be our ability to provide sufficient mass for the production of atomic fuel. This could be stored prior to the start or collected along the way. The latter method would consist of collecting cosmic dust, meteors and meteorites. For a trip of this short duration it would seem that this method would be unnecessary and that enough mass could be stored prior to the start. One obvious means of meeting this requirement could be to make use of some or most of the energy radiated by the sun during this considerable period of time, and to store it as mass. Although I have neither the knowledge nor the skills necessary to make even a rough calculation of the energy needed for this purpose, or the amount available from this source, I would nevertheless, venture a guess that a small proportion of the sun's radiated energy collected over a small percentage of the time prior to this move, would prove to be entirely sufficient. This would in all likelihood be the case even should it prove necessary to sustain this trip for a period of 100 years or more, until a satisfactory location is reached. The difficulties involved in getting satisfactorily established with our planets in orbit around a new sun — unless some better arrangement is discovered in the meantime — would surely be quite small compared to those already overcome.

Regarding the movements of our planets away from the sun, I might at this time point out what would seem to be a rather obvious method whereby this change could be delayed for a considerable period of time, although it would have to take place eventually. This method would consist of gradually moving our planets away from the sun in the period during which it becomes a nova, and maintaining a distance such that the radiation we receive from the sun would remain at a more or less constant level at all times. After a period of time the movement back to our present position could begin as the sun cools off. A further movement towards the sun would become necessary when the sun goes into its final decline. The time would, of course, come when the trip to another star would be unavoidable, but this might be delayed by several billions of years.

Prior to making the move referred to above, and possibly several billion years before that event, the human race would most surely be concerned about the next following move. Just how serious this next move would be is something which depends upon the outcome of the controversy — if I may call it that — concerning the red shift. If it transpires that this red shift does indeed indicate a rapid expansion of this portion of the cosmos, then a very serious move would be required. In this case the period of possibly somewhere between 10 billion and 15 billion years would be available before another and tremendously greater move would be necessary. Most of this intervening time would, in all probability, be needed for the collection of energy.

This change in location would be necessary, not only for the purpose of getting away from our galaxy, but also of leaving the whole group, which would by then, be rushing together in the process of forming another super-explosive situation. A course would have to be taken across the extremely large space between the group left behind and one which had more recently exploded, and therefore likely to be one in which a satisfactory home for our planets could be found—one which would last for a large number of years. Under these circumstances, a moving time of probably a billion times as long as the previous, and relatively minor move, would be required. Whereas the former one may have taken ten years, this major change in location would take something more like ten billion years.

As to the matter of energy required for an undertaking of this magnitude, it is clear that, despite the amount collected at the start, by far the greater part would, of necessity, have to be collected along the way. For what would likely be the major portion of this great journey we might well be dependent upon cosmic dust, meteors and meteorites, mentioned previously. It would be necessary, and entirely feasible, to collect material of this kind from great distances on all sides as the travel continues. At the same time we must not overlook the possibility that, during the intervening years, wholly new concepts based on new scientific knowledge may have evolved, just as dissimilar from our present concepts of science as were those of 50,000 years ago. Should that be the case, there is a strong likelihood that much larger sources would be readily available, which would obviate many, or most, of the difficulties which I foresee at present from this extremely long-range view. In any case, upon reaching the bordering group of galaxies, the process would begin all over again, but with the probability of each further move becoming less difficult with our increasing knowledge and experience.

A method suggests itself whereby this seemingly necessary long move could be avoided. The magnitude of this concept is such as to boggle the mind of even the most imaginative of the present day. We must, however, remember that we are attempting to conceive events which may take place no less than ten billion years in the future. And it may well be that occurrences which seem to us at this time to be nothing less than completely fantastic, could be accepted as commonplace long before that far ahead period. This concept is nothing less than the control of our entire galaxy. Actually, when this far distant time arrives, I have not the slightest doubt that we will no longer be working in isolation, but will be in closest harmony with many others, superior to ourselves. But, for reasons already stated I have to assume that we will be entirely alone. To continue within these guidelines, it seems obvious that, should our galaxy prove to be controllable, we could steer it away from any possible explosive situation and remain with it until such time as it expires. At that time, and provided that we are unable to reverse the aging process of this immense body, a move could be made to a younger galaxy. Should such a manoeuver prove to be feasible, it would facilitate the whole process very considerably.

Let us suppose now, that the theory which I am inclined to favor regarding the red shift proves to be correct, then the matter would be much simpler. In this case we could remain for a much longer time within our present galaxy by making relatively short trips from an old star to a younger one until such time as this galaxy is too far in decline to support us. At that point, a move would be necessary no farther than to the next suitable one. In the event that a whole galaxy is controllable as suggested above, then it would appear to make little or no difference which of the theories proves to be correct, but should galaxies remain uncontrollable the difference would be great. In the latter case, when a move to another galaxy becomes necessary, it would require a trip of almost certainly not more than a billion years, instead of ten times that amount, as mentioned. I feel that I have, as outlined previously, reason for supporting the aging theory of light rays, but this is something about which nobody can be sure at this time. In this respect it is similar to a great many other obscure matters about which many of us are disposed to ponder.

I have been attempting for the greater part of my life to get my thoughts concerning the subjects under discussion into some sort of order. This laborious task was originally begun and was continued entirely for my own satisfaction for many years before I had the slightest thought of putting any of it on paper. The latter undertaking also, is being carried forward primarily for the same purpose. As a result of all of this arduous pondering over a period of more than four decades, I have come to conclusions which I am attempting to explain here.

It may seem to my readers that I am blithely dismissing problems of huge difficulty and complexity as mere trifles. Such is not the case: I feel that I am aware, in a general way, of the inherent nature of these problems. My contention is that each one of a tremendous number of obstacles will be overcome in the fullness of time, and sometimes a very long time, by the diligence and skill of the best brains of the race. It may also appear that at times I am inclined to take a pedantic attitude. If any such overtone has crept into anything I have said, it has been quite unintentional. For a person, or a combination of persons, even the most learned, to adopt such an attitude at this time in our history would be nothing less than preposterous. For one such as myself it would be infinitely more so.

In setting out my views on the manner in which our race could survive throughout the coming eons, I may be in error in many of my conclusions. Some may be overly optimistic, with the difficulties to be encountered proving to be far greater than any which I can foresee. On the other hand, the advances in science and in our knowledge generally cannot very well be overestimated. Our race is still in its early infancy, and an almost total of the ultimate in knowledge, wisdom and skill is waiting for us somewhere in the future.

Such small amounts as we have acquired up to this time are at best no more than a small drop in a large bucket. Possibly a better comparison would be that of a cupful in the ocean. What I have tried to do is to establish in my own mind the utmost limits of that which can be achieved in the distant future.

Circumstances at that far time may well be such as to be quite beyond human imagination. I am merely trying to make some sort of an estimate, as best I can, of our final attainments, with the limited amount of knowledge available now. By this, I do not mean to suggest that I possess all of this knowledge. However, as I tried to point out previously, this very lack of knowledge, or at least a lack of anything more than a general outline of this knowledge, may be something of an advantage to me in this little task to which I have set myself. As stated previously, the real advancements will be made by those who are the top experts in each of the fields involved in each particular advancement. Actually my objective in this discourse is to try in some way to channel the thinking of our race into this direction.

At this point I must ask myself a question which is really nothing more than rhetoric, and which permits, in the main, only one answer. The question is this: assuming that we have reached the state of near perfection described above, and are beginning to approach our final goals in wisdom and knowledge, what would be our attitude toward a civilization which was just beginning to show signs of emerging? The answer would, of course, have to be that we would do anything and everything within our power to assist this new civilization in its development. Just what steps we should take in this direction is a matter of conjecture. My assumption here is that we would act as one, and that our intentions toward it would be nothing but the best. The obvious answer as to how best to rescue them when each has risen to a state above that of an animal, would be to lift them out of their condition of suffering and despair, into one of virtually perfect and infinite life, such as our own race would have attained. It might well seem to us now, at this period of our evolution, that any other course would be nothing short of demonic and entirely unworthy of our position of eminence, by that time achieved. As we become more advanced, I would think that the fallacy of this position will become more clear. It would appear to be more to the advantage of a developing race for them to be allowed to continue the working out of their own destiny, with all of the torture, wrongs and terror similar to those evident in our present situation. My reason for this opinion is that they would not be ready then, just as we are not ready now, for any such instantaneous advancement. No such promotion should be considered until they have worked their way up out of the jungle, adopted a respectable ethical norm, and have become very much more a truly civilized society than we are at this present time.

Prior to their arrival at this more advanced state, it might be profitable for them, as a developing people, to be given a little help occasionally, without the realization on their part that such aid had been given. When we consider this question we must take cognizance of all of those unfortunate individuals upon whom fate seems to have taken a most terrible toll. We all know of many such cases—whose lives contain nothing but sorrow, sadness and pain from beginning to end. What I am saying must not be taken as an assertion that these lives are to be completely and for all time abandoned. Any such suggestion would be quite unthinkable.

A point which should be made here is that this process of evolving into a society with ethical and intellectual standards of a passable nature, would seem to them, as it seems to us, an extremely lengthy procedure, The many thousands of years required are indistinguishable from all future time in the minds of most people of our race, and with a more recently emerged people it would be even more the case. In point of fact, the thousands of years mentioned amount to only a very brief minute when viewed from a different perspective of time.

Near the beginning of this discourse, I dwelt at some length on a topic which I chose to call "mind reading". (The first draft of that chapter was written in 1962, which is over twelve years behind me now.) This subject, or something akin to it, becomes important now when we consider the means by which we are to assist any emerging civilizations at some future time. The manner in which we would be able to recover these individuals, and, in fact all individuals of some particular race, including those who will perish prior to the time when their lives become infinite, is a matter which I must consider now. In the chapter referred to I made some mention of how this sort of thing might be possible by means such I am able to envisage now. It is quite possible that such methods will have become entirely obsolete at that far distant time, and other ways of accomplishing this end will be available. In saying this, I realize that it may seem as though I am guilty of a gross over-simplification. As pointed out a few pages back this is not at all true. I feel sure that I understand, in a general sort of way, the enormity of an undertaking of this kind. At the present time it is utterly impossible, and would, in fact, appear to the best brains now living in our civilization, to be quite out of the question for all future time. In considering matters of this kind we are all prone to think of them within the concept of tools and methods which are available now. While we all understand that these tools and methods are far from their ultimate in refinement and precision, still they are of a type which we can envisage. We have difficulty in contemplating that there may be others of an entirely different and immensely more intricate nature available to us at some distant time. I am quite sure that this weakness applied to me at the time when the chapter which I mentioned, was written. (It probably still does to a slightly lesser extent.) During the intervening twelve years I have not, I most fervently hope, stood still intellectually. It seems to me now, at this slightly later date, that we must take a different view and assume that greatly advanced tools and methods, about which we have no conception now, will be available at that remote time, which I would guess to be several billions of years away. We are just now entering into the era of automation and computation. It is agreed, and is indeed self-evident, that the usefulness of these instruments is limited only by the capability of the human intellect. These tools are now only in their early state of development, but there is no doubt that they will, sometime in the future, be totally capable of doing any job or solving any problem which is understandable by the best human minds. These jobs will include physical tasks much too small and intricate for human hand. And these tasks will be accomplished with a speed which will become virtually instantaneous. Some of these jobs could be of such complexity as to make them impossible by any other means.

In my discussion of mind reading of twelve years ago, I seem to have implied that this could be done only by means of radiated waves, including light, heat, electro-magnetic or any other: and that they could be reflected or originate from within. It appears to me now that this implies an unwarranted assumption; which is that no entirely new means of accomplishing this end will be acquired during the eons of time between the present and some billions of years in the future. I am now very much inclined to doubt this assumption for the reason that to me it is inconceivable that our knowledge and understanding of any subject has even begun to come remotely close to reaching its final limits. I would, in fact, say that the portion yet to come is so close to being the whole as to make the level of knowledge which has now been achieved seem insignificant, and that other enlightenment of tremendously greater value will be discovered in the course of time. These new findings will surely prove to be just as completely unknown to us, in our present state of profound ignorance, as were electro-magnetic waves about 40,000 years ago. In expressing this view, I do not think that I am in any way over-stating the case; actually, it is more likely that the reverse is true.

It may be pertinent to discuss the subject of Extra Sensory Preception at this point. There has been a vast amount written and spoken on this subject during the past few decades and I have no doubt that for the most part it consists of rubbish. For instance, a few years ago I purchased a book on the subject and read a portion of it. The point at which I lost interest was where the author recounted an ESP occurrence which was supposed to foretell the assassination of the late President Kennedy. The message which some person was said to have received prior to that tragic event was to the effect that this crime was to be perpetrated by one lone individual whose initials were "H.O." Obviously, the sender of this message had not the slightest idea of what he was talking about. The same thing applies to the author of this ESP book. It must be clear to any person of a little intelligence that the "H.O." (Harvey Oswald, of course) referred to in this book had about as much to do with this vile deed as did I. One would think that any information transmitted in this way should be based on factual knowledge, but I cannot say that I know of any evidence which would substantiate this view. It may be that this phenomenon does not distinguish between sense and nonsense. But be that as it may, it is clear that as soon as the rubbish has been stripped away, there remains a hard core of experience which can be explained in no other way.

It may be worth recounting that I myself was a part of such an experience quite a number of years ago. In the year of 1930 two of my younger brothers, aged 22 and 19 at the time, decided, against the strongest advice, to purchase a canoe and some camping equipment and to proceed to paddle down the Athabaska River and well into the Northwest Territories, a distance of over 1000 miles. Their intention was to remain in the Territories on a more or less permanent basis and to make their living by running trap lines. As neither of them had at that time any experience whatever which would qualify them to undertake such a journey, the proposition seemed somewhat foolhardy. But, as we other members of the family had no plausible excuse for having them confined to a mental institution, all we could do was to see them off and wish them well. They proceeded on this adventure, leaving by canoe from a place about 100 miles north of Edmonton, on July 1st, 1930. We did hear from them a few times from not too distant points for a few weeks, but after that—nothing. This circumstance was not unexpected since those were the early days of bush flying, and the mail service to the Territories was uncertain, to say the least.

    I suppose that all of us were worried about them, more or less—probably more. Certainly this applied to me, and I have no doubt that it applied to my mother more than anyone else. At Christmas of that year I spent a few days at Calgary with my mother and several of my other brothers and sisters. Occasionally, during this festive season, one of us would speak in a manner supposed to be jovial and light-hearted, masking our feelings of uneasiness, about the possible whereabouts and well being of our northern adventurers. A few days later I returned to the place where I was working at the time, the town of Camrose, Alberta, which is about 150 miles from Calgary. There while engrossed in my work, I had no further thoughts of my younger brothers for several weeks, although they were never far below the conscious surface of my mind. On a Saturday night at about the middle of January, 1931, I went to bed in a rooming house where I was staying at the time. During that night I was subjected to the most unusual dream which I have ever experienced. In this dream I saw my mother at a distance which seemed to be possibly twenty feet, and there was absolutely nothing else visible. I remember everything about it with complete clarity as I had reason to recall it very soon. My mother looked at me with a pleased expression and said, "You'll be glad to know that we've had a letter from Stanley and Dixie. They are quite well and they have fallen in with an experienced man and will be working with him during the winter. I can give you the address where you can write to them." That was the end of the dream. I do not know how much time elapsed until my next sensation, either dreaming or awake; it may have been a few seconds or a few hours, but it consisted of my being awakened by a knock at my door. When I answered I heard the voice of my landlady; "Mr. Turner, you are wanted on the phone." When I answered the telephone I heard the voice of my mother speaking from Calgary. She repeated to me word for word the message which I had received previously by other means. The only difference was that this time she gave me the name of the man with whom they were associated, and also the address at which I could reach them.

I cannot possibly shrug off an experience of that kind. This, plus accounts of many similar events obtained secondhand from reliable sources, would seem to indicate most positively that the human mind is capable of sending and receiving messages by means of which we have no understanding at the present time. I have no doubt that this, and probably many other mental capabilities, will be fully understood and will prove to be useful at some distant time, in connection with getting information concerning the human mind.

In any case, I do not think that it is too much of a strain to imagine this vision becoming a reality at some distant time and by whatever means. When that time comes, possibly several billion years hence, we will have the ability to extend a tremendous amount of help to some new race which, at that time, will be just beginning to emerge. When the time seems opportune, we will be able to pass on to them the records of their race which we will have been making since their beginning. With this information, which by that time they will have advanced far enough to be able to use, they will be capable of recreating all of the members of their race who have perished since its origin. As difficult—or as completely impossible—as this task appears to us now, it consists, when reduced to its simplest terms, of doing nothing more than copying something which is already in existence. Looked at in this way, it appears to be something possible of accomplishment. I do not doubt that we will prove equal to the job when the time comes.

When I first began to consider this matter seriously—possibly some thirty odd years ago—I would have thought that the above remarks were altogether too optimistic and rose tinted to be worthy of any serious consideration; and would have sounded too much like wishful thinking. When I say this, I mean that to me it would have sounded this way. More recently I have come to slightly different conclusions, as outlined below. In discussing what I would deem to be the best course for our race to take during a very long period ahead—although there may be any number of other and perhaps better courses available, and I may be quite wrong in any of my assertions—I have, as mentioned previously, deliberately taken the false assumption that we would be acting quite alone and without any assistance at all from any direction. This assumption implies that we are the first intelligent life to arise, and also that, even if others have arisen subsequently, they are far behind us in development. Any such conjecture is quite preposterous and is most surely not the case. In actual fact, there can be no reasonable doubt that an enormous number of such races have risen to a position not much less than infinitely superior to ours during the countless eons of the past. My suggestions as to what might be the future of our race were made for the purpose of attempting to determine what had happened previously in a huge number of other cases. It follows then, that we must certainly have been receiving whatever assistance deemed to be most advantageous to us in the final analysis, and also that we will receive more when the time comes that we have advanced to a state where we can be lifted entirely out of our present situation. In saying this I do not mean that we could be transported to a different location or anything of that nature: but only that we would be given whatever is necessary for us to complete the formation of something close to an ideal society.

After having reached these conclusions, I must now accept another, which would seem to me to be a certainty. This is that we have been under constant surveillance since the first emergence of life on this planet, and that a constant record is being kept now concerning everything on our earth, with particular attention to each individual of our race, and that this has been going on since man first started to evolve. Just what will be the result of all of this attention is, of course, impossible for any of us to predict with any assurance. It is conceivable that when each of us passes from this life we are immediately taken to some place far removed, where our lives continue under altogether different circumstances. I would think that this is somewhat improbable, and that it is more likely that as soon as we have advanced sufficiently, we will be given assistance in working out our own destiny. Forthcoming also at that time would be the individual records—or blueprints—of each of us. At this time, and with whatever help needed, we will be able to recreate all of our past members.

The arrival at this point on the road of logical conclusions, brings up a number of apparent problems, which, when examined with a little insight, turn out to be no problems at all. Possibly the most obvious of these, and the only one requiring any answer at all, is this: "Where are we going to put all these people?" The answer—inasmuch as it needs an answer—is twofold. First, with the advent of synthetic food, with changes made in this globe—including control of temperature and climate, the changing of water into solids, and the consequent large increase of land area—this earth could support possibly 10,000 times its present population. Second, we have the other planets and satellites of our solar system, as well as whatever additional planets we may require. These latter, we should have no trouble in taking from unused solar systems. Living space, it seems to me, should prove to be no problem at all.

I made the assertion in the second paragraph above, that we are at present, as we have been since the beginning of our race, under constant observation by a superior civilization: and I hinted at the same thing several times previously. Having to do with this assertion is the highly controversial and somewhat explosive subject of UFOs or "Flying Saucers". Arguments on this topic have been going on for at least the past twenty-five years. Some of the positions taken in this matter have been sane, sensible and objective attempts to get at the truth. Others have been quite the reverse. These discussions naturally include the scientific world, and it also appears to be somewhat divided on the subject. A number of scientists have gone to great lengths to play down the possibility of the existence of such things in order, apparently, to allay the fears of mankind regarding any danger from such a source. This, as I have tried to point out previously, is a fear which is widely held. Other, and to my mind, more objective scientists have taken a different view, and are willing to look into the possibility that there may be some truth in the theory that we do, occasionally have visitors from some far distant place.

As has been admitted or asserted by all shades of opinion in this controversy, as many as 90 per cent of the reports of supposed sightings of these unearthly objects can be explained as being nothing more than the figment of some person's imagination—some of these merely attempts at getting publicity and others sincerely mistaken—or the result of sighting objects which can be satisfactorily explained to be of earthly origin or phenomena. As has been noted by the more rational experts in this field, it is not with this 90 per cent that we should be concerned, but rather with the other 10 per cent for which there would seem to be no other explanation than that these vehicles are operated by intelligent beings from a distant civilization. That this place is located far beyond our solar system would seem to be a virtual certainty, for the reason that the possibility of two separate breeds of intelligent creatures located within such a small group of planets would appear to be extremely unlikely.

If the view is accepted that these vehicles actually are some sort of carriers containing intelligent beings—or, for that matter, unmanned vehicles controlled from distant points, or with such sophisticated equipment as to require no supervision—from a planet of a distant star (or elsewhere), then the question arises as to whether or not our sightings of them are made in spite of their efforts to prevent such sightings. Although I have never heard of any opinions being expressed one way or the other, still, judging by what I have been able to gather by implication, I would have to guess that most of the opinions of experts would favor the assumption that the evidence of these things which we have is obtained despite their efforts to the contrary. This is a view with which I would take exception. I think it most unlikely that those who control these space vehicles would have the slightest difficulty in preventing us from getting any evidence whatever that such things existed. To me it seems clear that what we have seen and what we know of these objects are nothing more nor less than that which they wish us to see and to know. Should they have wished to remain completely invisible and unknown to us, it is quite apparent that, with their extremely advanced knowledge and skill, they could quite easily have done so.

With regard to what their intentions are in these visits, we have very little evidence of any kind. They could be here merely out of curiosity. They could be here for the purpose of looking over the situation with a view to taking over the planet for whatever purpose they may choose and whenever they see fit. Or they may be here as I have suggested for our benefit. If the second of these suggestions is correct, I do not see any semblance of a reason why they could not have taken it over long ago, at any time of their choosing. There would seem to be nothing whatever that could be done by us to prevent such an occurrence, or which would cause them the slightest concern in doing whatever they happen to wish to this globe. I have to rule out this possibility altogether. That they are merely curious would seem to be extremely unlikely, as circumstances surrounding these visits appear to indicate a deeper purpose. I should imagine that if they wished nothing more than to see what was going on, a few visits spaced at long intervals would be sufficient for their purposes. Most of the information which they might desire could be readily obtained by some sort of telescopic device; and, should they wish further knowledge about this planet, then perhaps about one visit per millenium would be enough. As a matter of fact, there appears to be some evidence that sightings such as those reported within the last thirty years have been common throughout all recorded history. However, evidence of this type is vague and has been so blown out of all reasonable proportions by superstitious beliefs that very little credence can be placed in it.

Supporting the contention that these space visitors come here for our benefit from time to time—or are here constantly—is the unassailable fact that absolutely no harm whatsoever has come to our planet, its inhabitants, or its environment as a result of these visits. There have been many stories, some of which have a slight amount of credibility, about actual landings having taken place and of people having seen what they describe as little green men getting out of these vehicles. In a few cases people have even claimed to have been taken inside these vehicles by these little green men. I am inclined to put very little trust in reports of this kind, for the reason that their description of little green men is the stereotyped version of the appearance of intelligent life other than our own. I would be more inclined to believe these reports if the observers had described something altogether different. But be that as it may, and whether anybody has actually seen these beings or not, there is still some evidence that they have made landings on this planet, and have presumably gone to some pains to do so in such a manner as to avoid any harm to us. This evidence is not very substantial, but it gives at least a little substance to the theory that these creatures are here, as I have suggested, primarily for our benefit.

As I have tried to show, we are almost certainly under constant surveillance, and whatever information is needed by us will be delivered when the time is ripe. Naturally, this will be quite some time in the future, but not in any way approaching the billions of years which I mentioned as likely to be required for us to reach the ultimate in development, had we been left to our own resources. The time necessary for us to reach a position where we could profit from outside assistance, after having left our present semi-barbaric state far behind, and provided that we set ourselves to the task with a minimum of delay, could be as little as a few millenniums. By that time, assuming that we progress in a satisfactory manner, we should have achieved an acceptable sort of civilization. When that time comes, and when we have advanced sufficiently beyond that point, then I have no doubt that we will have the opportunity, and will be more happy to give whatever help we are able to provide in assistance to other emerging civilizations.

6 Some Thoughts on Religion

My infancy and boyhood, until the death of my father when I was fifteen, were spent as a member of a large family in a home which was, at least nominally, religious. My parents were at the time devout Anglicans. I really never did know exactly what my father's views were on religion. As a young man he must have had deep convictions on the subject. For a time, at that period of his life, he had serious intentions about going into the ministry, and had in fact done some studying in that direction. But this goal was abandoned after what I understand was a rather short time. The fact that he died when I was fifteen precluded the possibility of my ever having had any serious discussions with him on this or any other subject. I do recall him having lengthy discussions and arguments on the subject of religion with various visiting Anglican ministers, but I remember almost nothing of what I heard during these talks. One of the very few things of any substance which I do recall, occurred during one of these discussions when my father made the statement: "Any God who could see such a thing happening and, having the power to stop it, nevertheless refrained from doing so, must not be a God, but a devil." Even at that time when I was twelve or thirteen and had already divested myself of all religious convictions, as related below, it occurred to me that he was on rather shaky ground. I felt that if this was the entire basis of his skepticism—which I feel quite sure was not the case—then his doubts were not too well founded. I'm sure that he must have had a great many reasons which I do not now recall. Although something of a skeptic, he certainly had at least the remnants of religious convictions. I remember very well that he did not allow any card playing on a Sunday, and that he frowned upon many other games and frivolities on that day. Furthermore, he made sure that we all attended church as often as possible, and that his children attended Sunday school when such was available. He was, for the most part, a self-educated man, highly intellectual and very well read. In this respect, he attained a much higher level than anything I have been able to achieve. I rather suspect that during the last ten or so years of his life he was to a large extent coasting, and that his actions which I describe were the result of life-long habits. Although I am convinced that my father was more intellectual than I ever became, it is probably only fair to add that I do not think he had my complete independence of thought.

As far as my mother was concerned, she went along with him in all respects, exactly and unquestioningly, as long as he lived. I think I can safely say that her intellectual life began some years after his death in 1920, and after her large family had almost entirely grown up. It was at about this time that she became interested in serious reading, something which she had had no time for previously. This practice she continued with great profit to herself until her death in 1963 at the age of 94. During the last 30 years or so of her life. she abandoned religion completely, and died without any religious faith whatsoever, but at the time of my childhood she was a member of the Anglican church. As a matter of fact, following the death of my father, she made sporadic attempts to have us continue attending Sunday school, since she was convinced that in doing so she was carrying out my father's wishes. These attempts were successful for a few years, but soon most of her children had reached maturity and, as was inevitable, dispersed. An entirely new phase of my life started at the age of 17, and, in all the years since that time, I have been inside of a church for the purpose of attending a religious service just twice. My attendance on those occasions was due to the fact that in each case the minister conducting the service was a personal friend of mine.

The subject I am leading up to is the series of events which caused my complete abandonment of whatever faint religious beliefs I had at an early age. Until the time I was nine or ten I had, under the circumstances, absorbed the normal in religious teachings. Even at that time there were many things about these teachings which disturbed me, but which I thought would become clear when I understood more about the subject. I do not mean that I was in any way seriously disturbed, as my interest in the topic was no more than very small. My attendance at Sunday school started when I was about 10, and continued for a time on a rather hit and miss basis. It was as a direct result of these classes, and within a period of not more than one year, that I was stripped of every vestige of religious faith. The events concerning my Sunday school experiences which I am about to relate, and which were to have such a profound effect on my life, may very well not have been precisely as I will describe them. While I do remember exactly what my feelings were on each particular occasion, it may well be that many of the questions which I seem to remember asking, and the answers, or non-answers, which I received, may actually have not occurred except in my imagination. At these classes we had two different men teaching us at various times, but in my recollection I cannot now distinguish between them, as their beliefs and philosophies were identical, as well as I can recall. The classes I mention as having taken place when I was ten were the important ones for me. While I did attend other Sunday school classes on a haphazard basis until the time I was about 16, they were, as far as I was concerned, of no account whatever; and, for all the effect they had on my thinking and beliefs, I may as well have attended a series of sheep shearings.

From the point of view of either of my Sunday school teachers at that critical period which I mention, I must surely have been the world's worst and most completely unsatisfactory pupil. In spite of their best efforts, they were quite unable to prevent me from asking the wrong type of questions. The proper questions would have been those asked by good little girls. For instance: How many times a day should I pray and at what times? How long at a time should I pray? In what position should I be and how should I hold my hands? Supposing I am sick in bed and unable to kneel? What else must I do in order to remain in good standing in the Anglican church? Supposing I continue to pray regularly, and to to church regularly, and remain a good Anglican all my life, what will be my final reward? Questions such as these were exactly what the teachers seemed to want, and they went into ecstasies in their answers, always with a glance in my direction, no doubt hoping that I would get the messaage. On the other hand, any questions which attempted to go to the heart of the matter were entirely beyond their competence, and as I recall now, their only response was to declare such questions to be sinful. It would have been just as sensible for me, at that time, to make an attempt at conducting a course in higher mathematics. I might have given entirely satisfactory answers to such questions as: How much are seven plus nine? What is twelve divided by two? What is four times six? Any questions much beyond these would have had to go into the sinful category. At that, I would not have been much more out of my depth in such an endeavor than were these unfortunate men in attempting to conduct a worthwhile Sunday school.

Here are a few examples of incidents which I seem to remember. In dealing with the subject of baptism, the teacher opened the matter by making the statement; "All of us were conceived in sin." This was an unfortunate way of putting it, but still the remark would have passed unnoticed if I had been considerate enough to have stayed home on that particular day, or more precisely, had I been allowed to stay at home—I most certainly never went of my own volition. But as far as that goes, it would have been much more comfortable for the teachers had I stayed away entirely. The statement about being conceived in sin brought forth from me the entirely innocent and quite natural question. "What is conceived?" At this point the teacher obviously realized his faux pas and was overtaken by embarrassment and confusion. His only reply, if it can be called that, was to bluster out that we must absolutely take his word about things like that, and we were to never ask such sinful questions. The sin was mine, of course, for having the audacity to ask such a sinful question. This left me with the understanding that being conceived was something so utterly horrible as to be almost unspeakable, probably like having whooping cough. But as far as the burden of sin was concerned, I can say quite truthfully that it rested upon me with unbelievable lightness. After spluttering for awhile about sinful questions, the teacher returned to the matter of baptism. He explained that all of our lives began in sin so grave and so enormous that without divine intervention we were all, without lost forever. But, hallelujah! hallelujah!!, there was a simple and easy solution to the whole apparent disaster! All that was necessary was for us to go through the easy process of being baptized, and we were immediately cleared of all sin.

I had, on a few previous occasions, witnessed baptisms without any marked degree of interest or enthusiasm. It had been explained to me—without any request for an explanation—that it was not the few drops of water that did the trick, but rather the intercession on behalf of the infant by the right person, who was presumably in direct communication with the Almighty. At Sunday school we were given to understand that this business of baptism could be handled by an Anglican minister, but the question arose as to whether any other person had the power to intercede in this manner. The answer was somewhat confusing, but I gathered at the time that it must be done by some person with a "calling". Such a person could stand in for an Anglican minister, at least as far as baptisms were concerned. To me "calling" was something done to summon young calves and pigs to their feedings. It was something that I did regularly. I envisaged a man with a "calling" as one with a stentorian voice who spent most of his time running around the hills, valleys, plains and river banks of that sparsely populated area of southern Alberta, bellowing and roaring at the top of his voice something about, "Come all who wish to be baptized and I will be glad to oblige. Satisfaction guaranteed or your money cheerfully refunded." It seemed to me that any person who would spend his time in this ridiculous manner must be one of the world's worst damned fools, particularly on windy days: there simply had to be a better method, and one which would leave him with a little voice left over for the odd baptism which he was able to drum up. Actually, I realized at the time that there was a misconception somewhere, because the impression which I had gathered was too preposterous to be taken seriously even by the teacher.

On the subject of baptism I did have another sinful question about something which bothered me very much, and went about this way: what awful fate awaits those infants thoughtless enough or unfortunate enough to remain in an unbaptized state until overtaken by an untimely death? It seemed evident that such unfortunate events must take place occasionally. I envisaged a very ill and newly born child whose relations and friends were dashing around in all directions looking for an Anglican minister or listening for this character "calling", in a desperate attempt to obtain a baptism for this unfortunate child before it was too late. As I anticipated, the response was that once again I had been guilty of a sinful question. By that time I was getting to be an extremely sinful child, but this did not cause me any great amount of concern.

The matter of the Flood was taken up. No doubt we had all heard of this legendary event; certainly I had, and I remember very well my reaction of wonderment about the idiocy of the thing. We were told that the entire human race had become so utterly wicked and corrupt that God, in his infinite wisdom, had decided to wipe out the complete mess in order to make an entirely new start. He did pick out a few of the least unworthy, in order to carry on the race, and presumably to save himself the trouble and toil of creating man all over again. Those spared from the catastrophe were, of course, Noah and his family. My question about this affair was: "Aside from this little group, were there not in all the human race from Adam down to Noah, at least a few worthy of being saved?" Once again I received a non-answer. It was pointed out to me that, in all of the centuries of Christianity, the theological scholars had come to the unanimous conclusion, after pondering the subject exhaustively, that all of these people were indeed condemned to everlasting hell. Who then, was I to question such profound judgment? Well, I was not very much (and still am not) but I was enough to form my own opinion, which was that the formation of the philosophies of Christianity must have been in the hands of a bunch of idiots, and I was quite disinclined to accept their verdict. Although my views on the matter were unspoken, still my question itself caused me to be even more deeply mired in sin.

As is the case with all Christian churches, by far the most important subject was that of the coming of Jesus. We were told that he was God's only begotten son (whatever "begotten" meant I had no notion whatever, and did not ask as it seemed not important enough to be worth having another load of sin heaped upon me) and that he had been sent to save us from our sins. Without this intervention there could be no possible hope for any of us. In my mind this seemed to indicate that the haphazard and heavy-handed means of ridding the world of sin by the flood and its total extermination had been a complete failure and that the human race was no less sinful following that event than they had been prior to it. This in turn indicated that the Almighty did not have quite as much power as we had been led to believe. In my opinion at that time, any God as all-knowing and as all-powerful as he was supposed to be would never be in any way connected with such a complete fiasco as the flood evidently turned out to be.

I wondered also—and in fact asked a question—about the fate of all the people who had lived following the flood and before the advent of Jesus. My answer was exactly the same as it had been before; a rather embarrassed indication that such questions were sinful, and that, unfortunately all of these people, every last man-jack of them, had been judged unfit for salvation, and had been eternally damned. Once again, this seemed utterly ridiculous to me, but as I recall now, I had sense enough to keep my mouth shut about it. Presumably God had learned the futility of trying to free humanity from sin, for with the coming of Jesus he appears to have given up the idea altogether. It was obviously replaced by one whereby our sins, of whatever dimensions we cared to make them, could be readily forgiven, provided that we asked for the intervention of Jesus in the prescribed manner. I gathered that we were permitted to sin as grievously and as often as we might see fit, as long as we took care to clean out the manure from the stables of our souls frequently enough to prevent them from becoming too messy. This could quite easily be done by such methods as regularly attending Holy Communion, after which we would be completely free of all sin until such time as we had accumulated another mess. It is evident that I was becoming more and more disillusioned at every Sunday school session.

A question which bothered me more than any I have mentioned, and which was not touched upon at our Sunday school, was that concerning the very existence of God, as I had heard many people express such doubts. We had been told that the Bible was the word of God, and I had previously accepted as truth that it had been actually written by a supernatural hand—presumably the hand of God. Sunday school sessions brought out the fact that this was not at all the case, and that it had been written entirely by human hands, supposedly under divine guidance. To me, this was a horse of an entirely different color, and one with which I was not at all satisfied. Although I made no mention of this at Sunday school, I do recall that I brought the matter up with one of the teachers in a private conversation. Under these circumstances he was much more reasonable and less inclined to splutter about sinful questions. My question to him was to this effect: "Knowing the doubt in the minds of many people, why does not God take steps to remove the possibility of any such doubt, after which belief would be unanimous and the world would be a much better and less sinful place?" It was during his attempt to answer this question that I realized the truth of the matter. The mentioning of the subject had evidently caused him some embarrassment, and while he was making unsuccessful efforts to explain away my doubts, it struck me suddenly that he was actually much more disturbed about the matter than I was, and that he would probably have given everything he had in the world together with nine-tenths of his life if God would only come forth in such a way as to make any further doubt impossible. After he had completed his attempt at an explanation, which really did not answer my question at all, I had no further questions on this subject to him or to anybody else. I had come to the inevitable conclusion that the whole thing was entirely fictitious and resulted from nothing more than wishful thinking. The lesson I learned through this series of experiences was much more profound than I realized at the time. Briefly, it is the lesson of independence of thought. It is that when all propaganda and all instructions as to what must be accepted, along with any resulting impressions have been cast aside, and the matter examined critically, then it very often ceases to hold any mystery whatever, in the light of logic supported by established facts.

The same general rule holds true for events which have transpired in recent years. I refer here particularly to the assassination of President Kennedy. Following that tragic event, virtually no end of money was spent, efforts were made, and crimes committed by a group of extremely wealthy and influential people in an effort to mold public opinion into the belief that no conspiracy existed. When these people, with all of their massive resources, attempted to put the pieces together in such a manner as to present the picture of a lone and demented assassin, the results were so clumsy and the pretense so obvious that the whole thing was utterly unbelievable, and even ludicrous. When these same pieces are put together by any person with a modicum of intelligence and with complete honesty, the picture which emerges is quite clear and believable even though some of the pieces are missing. It was unfortunate for the above-mentioned conspiracy that most of the pieces were within the public view; had it been otherwise their chances of success would have been much greater. If this same principle is applied to the ongoing furore (as of January, 1974) concerning a more recent incumbent at the White House, it is not at all difficult to see where the guilt lies.

After having become an unbeliever at that early age, and having remained so ever since—certainly as far as religious beliefs go—it might seem somewhat ironical that, after a life-long study of the subjects covered by these discussions, I have been forced to the conclusion that there actually exists a super power of such a magnitude that it could be, in the broadest sense of the word, considered to be God. The present day religious conception of God is that of a single individual, merciful, benign, forgiving, all-knowing, omnipotent and ubiquitous; but one who, nevertheless retains some of his pagan characteristics of vanity, jealousy, sternly demanding respect of the genuflecting type and susceptible to the most lavish flattery. The super power, which I do not wish to refer to as God, and which I have shown—at least to my own satisfaction—to exist, is quite different. I would think it more likely that this power is a natural outgrowth of its environment rather than its creator. It is composed of, not one individual, but a close approach to an infinite number of individuals working as one in complete harmony and unanimity, obviously without any of the pagan characteristics, some of which are mentioned above. It is undoubtedly forgiving, merciful and benign, but possibly not completely all-knowing, not completely omnipotent nor completely ubiquitous. It would, however, approach these three qualities so closely that for all practical purposes it could be so considered.

An understanding of religion, its reason for being and its effect on humanity, may be obtained by a perusal of that great work by J.G. Frazer, *The Golden Bough*. I would think that this work is, without a doubt, the most important ever done on the subject. Its writing occupied some thirty years of Frazer's life, and it was completed in 1922. Since that time it has been a standard to which other writers have referred for reliable information on the history of religious thought. Even in its abridged version, it constitutes a rather large volume.

In this book, the course which religion has taken from earliest times about which we have any knowledge whatever, down to the present, is traced with meticulous care. Frazer explains how early man attempted to influence the supernatural beings which he supposed existed in almost every object around him, for the purpose of assuaging his fears and gaining favors. Usually he tried to coerce these various gods into seeing things his way by the use of sundry kinds of magic; but sometimes more forceful methods were resorted to. In these latter cases, the object which was supposed to embody some sort of a god, was threatened with the most dire consequences should he be foolish enough to refuse whatever request may have been asked of him. Eventually, over a long period of time, man came to the realization that such methods were to no avail, and that no worthwhile god was to be moved by magic or any form of coercion. It was found that man had no control over whatever supernatural powers which might exist, but that he must resort to humbling himself before it, him, or them, as the case might be, in the most abject fashion, and attempt to wheedle whatever favors he was seeking by flattery. The pagan beliefs and rituals which are still adhered to at the present time, and which have no place whatever in any Christian religion, would seem to have originated following this change. Some of the more easily recognized of these pagan rituals and beliefs are: holy communion; the belief in the virgin birth and immaculate conception; the acceptance of a vain, jealous and vengeful God, who must be approached on bended knee and flattered outrageously; who insists on being recognized as the sole and absolute monarch, and that the slightest variation from any of these concepts is nothing less than sacrilege.

At the end of this great work, Frazer indicated that in his opinion this type of religious cajolery or of attempting to gain favors from God by supplication was, in turn, giving way to another and altogether different sort of coercion. The suggestion here is that man is once again trying to influence the course of events himself and by doing so he is setting out to gain things, through his own efforts, which he had formerly tried to coax from a reluctant God. Instead of trying to accomplish this end through magic, as was the case in past ages, he is now attempting to do the same things by scientific means. This is obviously a most reasonable conclusion.

A study of this immense work will reveal a vast amount of pertinent and useful information. For myself, I can only say that it has been an enormous help to me in reaching my conclusions. I take the liberty of listing below a few of the salient points which have been of extreme importance to me.

It is shown that throughout all history man has been incapable of facing the uncertainties of this life and of anything which might follow, without the aid of some sort of intellectual crutch. In each case one of the many varieties of religion filled the need. The type of religion required has always borne a relationship to the state of advancement of the particular group served by this religion.

It is easily ascertained that wishful thinking has always been a prime factor in the creation of every religion since man first became intelligent enough to feel any such need. Also it is clearly shown that all were filled with large amounts of emotion and superstition.

It is made clear that such things as holy communion were practiced long before the Christian era (sometimes in a barbaric form), and that the fairy tales of the immaculate conception and the virgin birth had been used on many occasions prior to the birth of Jesus. It is shown that the very nature of all of the many gods which were worshipped, changed drastically as human idealism was rising.

While not explicitly mentioned in Frazer's work, the various forms of paganism which have carried over into Christian religions are made apparent; for instance this same constant alteration in the characteristics of God. The Old Testament God was vain, jealous and vindictive, and, for these reasons, cannot be taken seriously at the present time, since none of us could possibly accept a God whose ethical standards are lower than our own.

Another way in which paganism exemplifies itself is in the manner by which God must be approached—on bended knee and with unctuous and fulsome flattery—if one is to have any hope of gaining favors. It is also made clear in the course of Frazer's work that the ritual of holy communion as originally practiced, actually consisted of the drinking of the blood and the eating of the flesh of a god who had been slain for this purpose. This gruesome ceremony was carried out in the hope of obtaining god-like characteristics by those taking part in the ritual. Remnants of this practice, in which the blood and the body of the god is partaken of symbolically, has been perpetuated down through the ages, and is still carried out by some Christian churches.

Another highly interesting, although somewhat less enlightening work on the subject is *This Believing World,* by Lewis Browne. In this book, Browne traces the courses of all of the important religions since the dawn of history, with particular emphasis on existing religions. In this work Browne seems to lean rather heavily on Frazer, although this is not to be wondered at in view of Frazer's position of predominance.

In spite of all the interest which this book held, the part which most impressed me was not much more than a footnote. It consisted of his largely unsupported statement that, despite all its faults, religion in all of its various forms, had saved the human race. Presumably his thought was that without religious beliefs, the human race would have remained in some sort of barbaric condition. This may be true, but for myself I cannot entirely agree with him. The need for religion has been made clear by Frazer, but whether this need was so vital that humanity would have perished or reverted to animalism without some such benefit is another matter. Judging from my own experience, I would say that the amount of religious conviction of any individual is, as a general rule, in inverse proportion to his ethical and intellectual standards. I must, however, stress that this is not always the case by a long way; I have known many deeply religious people whose standards—particularly their ethical and moral standards—where the highest. But at the same time I must also say that those whom I would consider the most worthwhile individuals, both ethically and intellectually, have almost invariably had about the same religious convictions as myself.

When I speak of persons with no religious convictions, I must be very careful to exclude those who blatantly affirm their "atheism". Usually this is nothing more than an assumed position, taken for the reason that the practice of any religion would be a severe handicap in their pursuit of completely hedonistic pleasures. This is the type of whom it is said that in an army before going into battle there are no atheists. This old shibboleth is, of course, quite untrue. I have personally, as has, no doubt almost everybody else, known many who have faced just such circumstances without making even the slightest move toward seeking help from religion. When it comes to this sort of crisis, none of us with any real understanding of the futility of religious beliefs, are in any way inclined to turn in that direction. To persons of this type, good morals and high ideals are an end unto themselves, and require no further justification. This is, I believe, the answer to those who ask, as we have all heard many times, "Were it not for my religious beliefs, what would prevent me from committing all manner of sins?"

While it may be true, as Browne suggests, that the race could not have continued to advance without some form of intellectual opiate, it would seem to me, nonetheless, that in all ages there have been sufficient numbers of completely honest and intelligent seekers after truth who could have carried our civilization through, in the event that all regligions had been discarded. But at the present time, this is surely nothing more than an academic point. The important thing is that we have arrived at our present position and must look to the future, using the past only as a guide.

The time has arrived when beliefs based on no more than faith, hope and wishful thinking can no longer be taken seriously. This would include all religions. The process of discarding such beliefs must now begin. These must be replaced by conceptions based on logic and reasonable conclusions.

7   What We Can Do Now

Prior to the time when we can honestly say that we merit assistance from outside sources, and before there can be any reasonable hope that it will be received, tremendous changes will have to be made in our social structure. When I say this, I mean the social structure of the entire world, and not that of any particular country. Long before anything of this kind happens, nations as such will have vanished and the whole world will have become one community. The prime factor in making any such social change possible is a fundamental change in each of us individually. Most parts of the world today embrace social structures which are based firmly upon the foundation of personal greed and self-indulgence. This condition is usually referred to as "freedom" by the wealthy minorities who effectively control these countries. The meaning of "freedom", for those who over-use and misuse the word, is simply the freedom to exploit: that is to say, their own freedom to exploit other people—either their own or those of weaker nations. This is, after all, the only freedom in which they are at all interested. Before any real progress can be made, these attributes—which, without doubt apply to a degree in all of us—must be completely discarded, and we must all work for the benefit of the whole human race, rather than for ourselves as individuals.

We must be conscious of the rights and welfare of others,

and care as much for the lowliest persons in the world as we do for ourselves. I have made the statement on occasion that in my opinion the social system of any nation or community should be judged, not on the average standard of living, but rather on the standard of living of the lowest one-hundredth of one per cent of the community involved. My position has been that this would give a more accurate indication of the true worth of that particular social structure. In the context of my present discussion, I find it necessary to go a step further, and to regard the welfare of the very lowest human of the entire race as the criterion by which to judge the value of our world-wide social system.

When I speak of self-indulgence, it must not be assumed that this term has anything in common with self-fulfillment, which, of course, is a different thing altogether. I am entirely convinced, and I am sure that all thoughtful and intelligent persons will agree with me, that those who have achieved the most toward self-fulfillment are those who have given most freely of their own time, energy and worldly wealth in attempting to better the cause of humanity generally, without any regard whatsoever for themselves. We must all emulate this type of individual before we can have the least hope of taking the first step toward any of our goals.

A few faltering steps are being taken toward the establishment of a better type of society by some nations at the present time. These attempts have met, and are meeting with at least a degree of success, and to that extent they are in the right direction. On the other hand, the great majority of the smaller nations are now at about the point of advancement as were our forebearers during the dark ages. This is as might be expected, and may not be of any great importance, since bringing about change in these out of the way places would appear to present very little difficulty, after the large nations have led the way and are well started down the road toward becoming an entirely united and much superior world. The alarming thing about the situation of the world at present, is the state of a great nation which, while making a show of pretending to favor social advancement, actually uses its utmost efforts in attempting to prevent or delay any such movement. The reference in this sad commentary is to our powerful neighbor to the south. This nation, while having a facade of democracy, is actually, in matters of real importance, governed by a wealthy and extremely influential minority dedicated to the preservation of the status quo at any cost. This minority, under normal circumstances controls, or virtually controls the entire government—legislative, executive and judicial—and seems to have power to take whatever decisions it chooses, even up to and including the assassination of presidents and of prospective presidents who seem disposed to threaten the aspirations of this small but powerful clique. Regarding this influential group, it must be noted that while they give a great deal of attention to preventing any social advancement in their own country, and consequently avoiding danger to their personal positions of power and wealth, they are not at all indifferent to social change in other parts of the world. In this connection they are ready at all times, to go to any kind of extremes, both overtly and covertly, to prevent anything which might be called a forward step in even the remotest corner of the world, when this end can be accomplished without too much danger to themselves.

A case in point is that of the utterly unsuccessful attempts by a malignant little group of Americans to oust the Castro government of Cuba. At times these attempts were so naive as to be almost laughable. Nevertheless, they would have encountered no great difficulty in replacing the Cuban regime with one more to their liking long ago, had it not been for an entirely justified fear of massive retaliation from Cuba's friends of gigantic size.

At the same time it has to be admitted that, should a substantial majority of Americans demand a change, then that change would be forthcoming despite all that the powerful minority could do to prevent it. This is the case even when such a change involves a drastic alteration in the national governmental policy. That there is a definite limit to the influence of this small group was made evident after years of intervention in the affairs of southeast Asia, when a complete withdrawal was made unavoidable by the weight of public opinion. This is a hopeful sign.

When I speak of the backwardness of this great country, I do not by any stretch of imagination, mean to infer that all of its citizens are backward. There are many millions—and in fact many tens of millions—of Americans who are quite well advanced in their social philosophies, certainly just as advanced as I am, and in a great many cases much more so. These are, of course, working in the opposite direction to that of the behind-the-scenes government, and I am certain that their aspirations will ultimately prevail. All of this serves to point out only one small part of the huge task before us which must be accomplished before we can hope to make even slight progress toward our goals.

Before leaving the subject of our American friends, I would like to mention the amusement which I derived early in 1974, from an article which appeared in a local paper about a noted Canadian who sprang to the defence of our good neighbor to the south. This individual is Mr. Gordon Sinclair, a noted, respected, highly accomplished, and wealthy journalist, radio broadcaster and television personality. The item in this local paper had to do with a broadcast made by Mr. Sinclair some months before, in which he deplored the verbal attacks being made at the time, on the U.S.A., with particular reference to those coming from Canada. If one is to believe Mr. Sinclair, the Americans are the most open-handed, generous-to-a-fault and entirely praiseworthy people of the entire world. In this broadcast he pointed out the magnanimous way in which they had built up the economies of Germany and Japan following World War II, and how they had on almost countless occasions gone to the aid of various communities of the world when the need arose. Mr. Sinclair said, if I remember correctly, that he could cite 5000 cases where

American aid had been dispersed in this noble fashion. I am not inclined to dispute this point since he seems to have an excellent memory. At the same time he defies anybody else to mention more than a very few (or was it any?) cases where the opposite was true; where aid had been bestowed upon Americans in their hour of need, from foreign sources.

Mr. Sinclair is a good, decent, honest and entirely upright man, and I have never entertained the slightest doubt that his intentions were the very best in this case, as they usually are. As previously noted he is a wealthy man, and this wealth has been amassed by himself as a result of his efforts in his chosen field. He writes and speaks with great skill, but in my estimation he occasionally has the habit of looking at his topics in an emotional manner. After all, his readers, listeners and viewers are much more responsive to an emotional approach than to a logical one. No doubt this accounts, in a large part, for his success. The impression he gives me is that he does not take the time, or that he does not have the ability—I'm not sure which—of thinking any complex subject through to its logical conclusion. It might be said that he gives the impression of going off half cocked on occasion. This could have been the case concerning the talk in question, since he admittedly compiled it on the spur of the moment.

In reply to Mr. Sinclair's statement, I would like to point out that, almost invariably, this American aid of which he speaks, goes to countries and parts of the world which this same American minority considers to be "safe". They do everything possible to prevent any of it from falling into the hands of a government which might be considered progressive in the true sense of the work, or one which seems likely to take any progressive step. The help which he mentioned as having been extended to Germany and Japan was bestowed upon them for the entirely pragmatic reason of preventing these countries from being drawn into the camp of the so-called "enemy"*—or the "other side"—about which U.S. officials are so prone to bluster. I think that it is true to say that American aid was given in great abundance to the military cliques in Greece and more recently in Chile for the assistance of these thoroughly corrupt and reprehensible conspiracies in taking over—in a completely illegal manner—the governments of these unfortunate countries. The same was true in the case of their most generous provision of help to the utterly corrupt government of South Viet Nam, which resulted in tragedy of catastrophic proportions within the last decade. I would advise Mr. Sinclair to look more closely into matters about which he is speaking. On this occasion he would appear to have been left somewhere in the deep outfield.

If I may be permitted to draw a parallel here, it would be that Mr. Gordon Sinclair's alacrity in protecting American honor is somewhat similar to a defense which I myself might make of a crime syndicate, in the event that it should be threatened and beset by a rowdy gang of kindergarten children.

Inasmuch as Mr. Sinclair is speaking of Americans individually, as opposed to the policies of their government—particularly that pertaining to their foreign policy as of early 1974—then he is quite correct in his assessment of Americans as being most open-handed, generous and altogether very fine people. This applies to the vast majority. The shortcomings arise from their being afflicted by the same gullibility which affects virtually all of the peoples of the world. And they have the disadvantage also, of having for long been the world's richest nation (which is still true) and of being until recently the most powerful (which is no longer true). In any case, it is not for Canadians to take a "holier-than-thou" attitude; I am sure that, had our positions been reversed, we would have taken just about exactly the same course as was taken by them. I feel quite sure, too, that in the not-too-distant future, these people will straighten out their affairs and become a much more progressive and altogether more worthwhile nation. Hopefully, of course, the same thing applies to all of us.

The tasks which must be accomplished by our race before we have the slightest chance of any worthwhile advancement are staggering, and if a short-ranged view is taken, one might well be inclined to throw up his hands in despair and declare the whole thing completely impossible. But on the other hand, in taking a long-ranged view, we must remember that our race is still in its earliest infancy, and that up to the present time we have made at least a small amount of progress. If this rate of progress is maintained, it is inevitable that future millenniums will take care of anything else which may be necessary for us in this long journey. The most immediate priority is the mere keeping of our race in existence while maintaining at least a small forward movement. In order to accomplish this end the reformation of each individual becomes vital, since it is not possible to build a superior society upon the present inhabitants of this planet. Each of us requires many improvements. A single-nation world is a prerequisite for the needed progress, and this appears to be impossible under the present circumstances. The chief characteristic of most of us at the present time, is that of greed, with the accompanying attitude of "I'm doing alright, so to hell with the rest of the world." We must get rid of characteristics and attitudes such as these, and come to realize that we must go forward as one if we are to make any progress at all. When this point of unanimity has been reached, we will be in a position to go forward with the certainty of being able to make good progress.

There has been a great deal of talk recently about how, in this "age of miracles", various devices have taken over most of the labor which was previously done by humans. The concern in some quarters is that with increasing automation, human toil will become less and less necessary, and as a consequence man will have much more leisure time. The question then arises as to how this spare time can best be utilized, and whether it will have a demoralizing effect on the race. To me, the question of too much time is one which should not arise; but if it does, it will be a problem of short duration. There is a tremendous amount of work of great importance which should occupy all of us far into the foreseeable future—certainly for as far ahead as I can possibly see. As soon as a better type of society has been developed the human race will proceed to organize itself, right down to the last individual, while a start is being made on the vast amount of research which is an urgent necessity. When a start has been made on these gigantic and almost numberless projects, any thought of more than a normal amount of leisure time will vanish. Under such circumstances as I foresee, no one of us will have the least desire for more spare time than we have at present, and any thought of reducing the working hours would not be seriously entertained. Indeed, I feel quite confident, that all of us will become so thoroughly engrossed in whatever part we are taking in the great overall scheme of co-ordinated research that we will become, as dedicated scientists always do, oblivious to the passing of time, and eager to work very long hours indeed at entirely our own volition.

A prerequisite to our making a beginning on the long journey to our destiny is for each of us to realize the futility of any mundane gains of a personal nature, which we value so highly at the present time. We must understand that the only acquisitions of a personal nature which have any real value, are those of the intellectual type. If progress is to be made, we must each of us recognize the necessity of going forward as a unit, and that the fate of each of us is inexorably bound up with the fate of the whole race. When this better state of society has been reached, as I am sure it will be, within the next few centuries, then the question of priorities as to the direction which the great thrust of research should take, will become a matter of importance. At that time, and with mankind organized to work as one, I have no doubt that these priorities will set themselves in order, and it will become clear as to the sequence in which these numerous and extremely difficult tasks are to be undertaken. I feel quite sure, too, that any advice on the subject which I might give at this time would prove to be redundant. However, since my purpose in writing this discourse is an attempt to influence the thinking of a few people of my generation, I take it upon myself to make a few observations as to what I consider would be the proper order of procedure at the time when certain priorities are needed by our society.

A matter which besets the human race at present, and which has done so for a good while in the past, is that of education. It would appear self-evident that problems in this area must be solved before we can contemplate a united world. Obstacles in this important field must be entirely overcome before we can take even the first step on our journey toward a higher type of society. The solutions to these problems are so obvious that I feel apologetic about mentioning the subject; still, a few remarks will at least do no harm. When we speak of education, we must differentiate between education and training. Both are obviously necessary and each individual should be given all the education he is capable of absorbing. Following that he can be trained in whatever line of research or whatever other endeavor in which he may be interested, and where he can do the most good. It follows naturally that when any person is engaged in the pursuit in which he can accomplish the most, and where he can do the most useful work, this is where he will be the happiest. This will be the case when our society has been properly reorganized, and is ready to take its first step in the beginning of its advancement.

During this entire discourse I have often (as in the case under discussion above) used the masculine pronoun. This has been done without in any way intending to confine its meaning exclusively to the male sex, or to insinuate that the tasks undertaken must be accomplished entirely by males—it could, in fact, and in every case be quite possibly accomplished entirely by females. I use the masculine pronoun in exactly the same way in which the word "mankind" is used; when every member of the human race is included.

Second to merely keeping the race alive and making a little progress, I would say that the next goal toward which our efforts should be directed would be that of making human life, while still in maximum health and vigor, ever and ever longer until eventually it becomes infinite. A more advanced and difficult part of this same undertaking will be that of devising methods whereby the makeup of each individual can be stored in such detail as to make possible his recreation in the event of his becoming lost through some misadventure. This last suggestion would seem, at the present time, to be nothing less than completely fantastic, but I am convinced that with the passing of centuries it will become less so. All varieties of research are important, and all must be given every possible encouragement; with special emphasis on scientific research. The acquisition of new knowledge in any direction, including that obtained with no other objective than the pushing back of our horizons, must be encouraged, and efforts along such lines always maintained. Knowledge is the foundation upon which has been built the advancement of our race during its short history, and I can foresee no time in the future when this will not be true.

All scientific achievement will eventually prove to be of great value. The field is wide open in opportunities for new discoveries in a limitless number of directions, and is filled with an equal number of challenges. The magnitude of the difficulties faced by those who would undertake these tasks certainly need no underscoring by me. But, however great the difficulties, all of them will be brought to successful conclusions during the countless ages ahead.

At some time in the future, and possibly in the not too distant future, when we have become a truly human society and have acquired sufficient technical knowledge, we will be given whatever assistance that we need to enable us to re-group ourselves with the inclusion of every last individual of our race who has ever lived up until that time. This assistance will be given to us by a super-civilization, or a group of super-civilizations, who have had us under their surveillance since life on this planet first began. At that time we will have the ability to continue our journey to ever greater achievements, while we constitute a civilization closer to perfection. In the course of time we may reach a point where we, in turn, will be able to give assistance to other emerging races on newer planets. It is toward this most worthwhile goal that we must work; each of us to the limit of his particular ability, talent and enthusiasm, for a tremendously important objective.